# Iron and Brass Implements
## of the English House

A SIXTEENTH CENTURY SURREY DOWN-HEARTH

# IRON AND BRASS
# IMPLEMENTS
## OF THE
# ENGLISH HOUSE

## J. SEYMOUR LINDSAY
D.C.M., F.S.A.

### ILLUSTRATED BY THE AUTHOR

### WITH AN INTRODUCTION BY
### RALPH EDWARDS
C.B.E., F.S.A.

LONDON / ALEC TIRANTI / 1964

*The Publishers wish to thank The Medici Society for their*
*courtesy in connection with the publication of this new edition*

FIRST EDITION WAS PUBLISHED IN 1927 BY THE MEDICI SOCIETY, LONDON
PRESENT EDITION REVISED AND ENLARGED, 1964

PRINTED BY PORTLAND PRESS LTD., LONDON W.1
BOUND BY MANSELL & CO. LTD., LONDON

MADE AND PRINTED IN THE UNITED KINGDOM

TO THE MEMORY

OF

# LEWIS GEORGE RUSSELL-DAVIES

KILLED IN ACTION IN THE GREAT WAR

21st OCTOBER 1916

# ACKNOWLEDGMENT

THE Author wishes to express his thanks to Mr. F. P. Barry for undertaking the indexing of this book: to Major C. T. P. Bailey, of the Department of Metalwork, Victoria and Albert Museum, for his kind assistance, and to the attendants in the Museum Library for their helpfulness.

For the extra examples in the American Section, my grateful thanks I extend to Mr. and Mrs. Carl Jacobs for organising the co-operation of American collectors ; to Mr. Charles F. Montgomery, Senior Research Fellow of the Henry Francis du Pont Winterthur Museum, Delaware, for sending photographs ; to Mr. Dean A. Fales jnr., Director of the Essex Institute, Salem, Mass., for photographs and valuable information; and to all those who have helped in this Section.

# CONTENTS

# INTRODUCTION

THIS IS THE FIRST BOOK written in English about domestic iron implements, once an important part of household equipment. They need elucidation, for many of them are mysterious objects. I have often regarded the collection at the Victoria and Albert Museum with something of the awe that attaches to the unknown—things all knobs, spikes, and catches, the very use of which would be withheld from me were it not for the labels. From Mr. Lindsay's standpoint that collection is still incomplete: the jacks and cranes which perform curious evolutions are scarcely represented, nor is there one of those fascinating contrivances for roasting meat with the co-operation of a dog. Mr. Lindsay has added to the number of rushlight holders and similar trifles that the Museum possesses; but these can be readily understood by the ignorant, and it takes something more abstruse to test his powers. He knows by a kind of intuition what was the original purpose of wheels, cogs, and pulleys, the whole baffling mechanism once deemed indispensable for the preparation of a really good dinner. From him one may learn, not only of the purpose, but of the style and character of domestic ironwork—the flourishes that proclaim an example German, French elegance expressing itself even in cooking accessories, the fitness for purpose so characteristic of England. The age when these things were produced was ignorant of the heresy that beauty is a luxury easily dispensed with. There was nothing too humble to have pains bestowed upon it. Ruskin noted the mediæval mason's prodigal expenditure of art on mouldings and spandrels too high to be seen: a similar principle guided the worker in iron who made skillets and pot-hangers beautiful for cooks and scullions. 'Put the porke on a *fayre* spete' directs a Cookery Book of about 1430; it meant only one clean and serviceable, but the phrase may stand as a symbol.

Examples of the obsolete armoury of the kitchen must be sought for in lumber shops and street fairs, for they have outlasted their usefulness. With them has gone much of the pomp and circumstance that attended the preparation of food—'Our roasting,' writes Madame D'Arblay in 1778, 'is not magnificent, for we have no jack.' People were then learning to do without them, but had not said good-bye to the time-honoured method. There was an attempt to give it a new lease of life, and in 1794 Mr. Whittington came before the public with a jack-driven 'Machine for Roasting Meat in a much superior manner to anything now made Use of for that Purpose.' In an age when labourers burnt hayricks rather than use the new machinery, Mr. Whittington's invention had small chance of approval in the kitchen.

But one large class of domestic ironwork has escaped this melancholy fate: andirons and firebacks will continue to be used in the ancient manner, while a few houses maintain the noble custom of burning logs. These are the aristocrats of the craft, destined for the Hall or Great Chamber and sometimes ornamented with their owner's arms. Among the most interesting are those commemorating events celebrated in national or local history. A Sussex ironmaster and his wife are burned at the stake under Queen Mary: a fireback representing their martyrdom is cast to minister to the element that consumed them! After the Restoration, another plate bears the Boscobel oak with crowns dangling from its branches and on a ribbon the initials C. R.

There is something very impressive about this metal. 'All things decay and wear out in time,' writes Bishop Sherburn early in the sixteenth century, when providing for the safety of his Cathedral library; yet iron is almost indestructible. Racks plunged into the oven countless times to clean clay pipes retain no trace of the fierce heat; the design is yet fresh and perfect on firebacks gnawed by flames through centuries.

Bronze has been used for domestic utensils from remote antiquity: it has, moreover, been the medium of much great art. When the bronze pots from Scotland (Part II, Fig. 111) were made is a matter for conjecture, but as they were found containing hoards of coins hidden in the fourteenth and fifteenth centuries it may be said of them that like the Urns of the immortal *Discourse* they have 'in a yard under ground . . . quietly rested under the drums and tramplings of three conquests.'

Brass and latten, more malleable substances, were favoured because they permitted of engraved ornament and could be cast in many shapes.

Latten to the lay mind is somewhat mysterious—there are few who could say off-hand of what it is composed. It is usually thought of as

2

akin to brass, but without its lustre. Yet it was once a synonym for brightness. Chaucer compares it with the Sun—

> 'Phebus waxe old, and hewed like laton
> That in his hote declination
> Shone as the burned gold.'

Of brass domestic utensils there was no lack in the Middle Ages. Sir John Fastolfe, whose redoubtable deeds at Agincourt give his inventory a peculiar interest, had, in that house at Caistor, so familiar through the *Paston Letters*,

> 'three grete brass pottys of Frenche making.'

The translators of the *Authorised Version* were not at pains to discriminate between metals and alloys—with magnificent licence, they make God promise his people a country 'out of whose hills thou mayest dig brass.'

Photographs are out of place in a work of this kind; you may get meticulous accuracy, but something indefinable escapes a mechanic process. Mr. Lindsay's drawings convey the artist's personal vision, and his sensitive line admirably renders the surface quality of ironwork. He has had a predecessor moved by the same enthusiasm. William Twopenny, early in the nineteenth century, wandered through England filling his sketch-book with many fine examples which have since disappeared. In Elysium his spirit will rejoice over the publication of Mr. Lindsay's book.

RALPH EDWARDS.

# PART ONE

# THE HEARTH

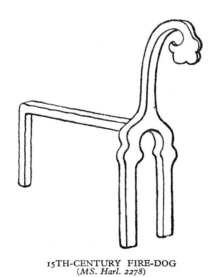

15TH-CENTURY FIRE-DOG
(*MS. Harl. 2278*)

PART ONE

# THE HEARTH

THE MOST PRIMITIVE FORM of fireplace in which metal work formed a part was the down-hearth. This was a slab of stone or iron slightly raised above the floor level upon which the fire was made.

Of the down-hearth there were two forms, the earliest being the central hearth, which was in use in the great halls down to the end of the mediæval period. The second is the wall hearth, the smoke from which was carried off by means of a flue built upon the face of the wall or through a cavity in the fabric of the wall. In many parts of the country, where wood fuel is easily obtained, this latter form of hearth still survives, especially in the older farmhouses and cottages.

Of the various articles connected with the hearth the fire-dog is the most primitive. The prototype is the Kelto Roman form of double-ended dog, examples of which have been excavated from time to time in various parts of England (Fig. 1). It should be noticed that this form is similar in construction to the large dog at Penshurst in Kent. The Penshurst example, illustrated in Fig. 2, is in the Great Hall which dates from 1350; the dog is later, being of the sixteenth century, and without doubt replaced one of similar design. This hearth occupies a central position, the smoke finding its way out through the roof. The dog is composed of two vertical bars or stems, splayed out at the base in the form of a cusped arch. These two uprights are connected by a heavy horizontal billet bar, supported in the centre by a leg which prevents the bar from settling down when rendered soft by the great heat. The central hearth, although the most primitive, was contemporary for many centuries with the wall down-hearth. Fire-dogs constructed for use with the wall down-hearth were single ended, and were used in pairs, the billets of wood being supported by the return or billet bar.

Prior to the introduction of cast iron at the beginning of the fifteenth century, dogs of wrought iron were in use in some of the large establishments throughout the country, but few have survived, and miniatures in illuminated MSS. seldom show dogs in use on the hearth until the fifteenth century. One example which occurs in an English MS. of the first half of that century is shown on page 5.

The earliest existing examples that form a distinctive class are the massive cast-iron dogs, dating from the late fifteenth to the seventeenth century. On many the decoration shows a curious blending of Gothic and Renaissance ornament. This class of dog is shown in Figs. 3 to 7. The first is a cast-iron dog of the early sixteenth century, with cusped arch at the base and stem finished in the form of a head.

The four cast dogs shown in Figs. 4 to 7 illustrate the Renaissance tendency. The earliest of these (Fig. 7) is dated 1575, and is quite free from Gothic feeling. Fig. 6, a dated example of the seventeenth century, bears the initials of Thomas Pelham, and upon a shield at the junction of the legs and stem the Pelham badge in its early form, prior to the addition of the strap. An uncommon feature in Fig. 5 is the wrought-iron hook cast into the face of the upright. This was for carrying a meat spit and is a type belonging to the early seventeenth century. The other example is of Gothic outline, with Renaissance details, dated 1667. The demi-figure was a fairly common finial in cast dogs of this period, and is illustrated in Fig. 8, which is taken from a drawing by William Twopenny in the British Museum. It is evident that these dogs (from Cobham Hall, Kent) were made for a particular fire opening, the pattern being cut to give more space between the dogs.

Of wrought-iron examples of the sixteenth, seventeenth, and eighteenth centuries there are two distinct classes, small dogs for supporting the burning embers known variously as brand-dogs, dog-irons, chenets, and 'creepers,' and a much larger and more important type, which stood close to the jambs of the chimney opening, their chief function being to support the meat spits.

The former class are shown in Figs. 9 to 13; 9 is Elizabethan; 10, 12, 13 are the typical seventeenth and eighteenth-century type; 11 is of wrought steel and belongs to the late eighteenth century. Some of the later period dogs have an upright spike on the return bar, showing it was used for supporting a grate. Such a dog is shown in Fig. 15. The two other examples shown (Figs. 14, 16) illustrate the last type of fire-dog, and have cast-iron fronts in the Adam taste with wrought-iron billet bars. These dogs were cast by the Carron Company, and during recent years have been recast, the only difference being that the name occurs on the back instead of the front.

8

Large wrought-iron dogs for holding the meat spits figure in sixteenth-century MSS.; but were probably used much earlier, and were usually termed 'andirons.' The name was applied to the more important fire-dogs and spit dogs, and occurs in an assessment for taxation of the year 1300 of goods belonging to Roger the Dyer of Colchester, 'I andiron pr. 3d.;' also, spelt more archaically, in an inventory of the effects of Sir John Fastolfe, who figures prominently in the *Paston Letters*. The following are enumerated in his house:

> 'Item j Aunderen—Item j Firepanne
> Item j payre of tongues.
> The utmost chamber nexte Winter Halle
> Item jj stanndyng Aundeinys.'

That the name 'andiron' was not applied to the small dog is suggested by an inventory of the Stock in Trade and Furniture of a Tavern in Bishopsgate Street in 1612 which specifies:

> 'Item one payre of iron andirons with four brasse knobbs and two payre of toungs and one payre of creepers 10/–.'

Again in the inventory of the effects of the Earl of Northampton, 1614, there occurs:

> 'Item two small creepers with brass toppes        iis vid
> Item two andirons topped with copper        iiis
> Item A fire shovell, tongs & creepers topped with brass        vis.'

And in 1656 the Rev. Giles More, a Sussex parson, paid 1/2/0 for

> 'A pair of brasse andirons'

and 5/6 for

> 'Two dogs with brass heads.'

Of the three spit dogs illustrated Fig. 17 has in addition a cup or cresset-like form at the top, which was for a candlestick, torch or holding a cup or mug during basting operations. The hook for holding the spit is adjusted by engaging on a ratchet at the back of the upright. The other two, Figs. 18 and 19, are the usual type of spit dog with hooks at the back of the stem for supporting the spit at various levels.

The chief drawback to the early wall down-hearth was the destruction of the back wall of the hearth opening caused by the fire. So great was the damage in the larger fireplaces, that the back wall had to be refaced

9

from time to time. This difficulty was overcome with the introduction of cast iron, which led to the production of large thick plates of sufficient strength to resist the heat. These 'fire-plates' or 'fire-backs' are still to be found in great variety throughout the country.

There were various methods employed for making the moulds from which these backs were cast, the most primitive being to make an impression in sand with a board the required size. The ornament, if any, was added by pressing small articles into the cavity made by the board. Almost any object of a convenient size seems to have been used, as there are instances of knives, forks, the palm of a hand, compasses, and small armorial devices.

This method of making fire-backs continued to the end of the seventeenth century, and is represented in Figs. 20 and 21. The first, dated 1642, bears the badge and initials of Thomas Pelham: the moulding surrounding the pattern from which this was cast shows more than usual care. The other example, dated 1685, shows the irregular method of using the movable stamp. Another fire-back (Fig. 22) belongs to this class and is of particular interest, being a relic of the now extinct Irish iron industry. It bears the arms of the O'Rourkes of Doromahair, the ancient chieftains of Breffin.

Fire-backs cast from one-piece carved patterns came in during the sixteenth century, but not to any great extent. The following century was the period which claims most of the one-piece carved patterns, and these may be divided into three classes—Armorial, Subject, and Dutch. The first group is represented by Fig. 23. It bears the Scottish Lion and Thistle supported by the English Rose and French Fleur de Lis, with the date 1649 and the initials I.M., this decoration suggesting it was cast to commemorate the death of Charles I.

Subject backs are shown in Figs. 24 and 25. The former depicts the ironmaster Richard Lenard, surrounded by articles connected with his trade. At the top is the inscription, 'Richard Lenard Founder at Bred Fournis,' and the date 1636. In the adjacent left-hand corner of the panel is a shield quartered, bearing a hammer, plummet, iron-weight, and pinchers or tongs. Below this is a brick built smelting furnace with flames issuing from the top; at the right-hand side are a tankard and a chalice upon an ornamental bracket; below a fire-back, the initials R.L., and a lozenge.

Fig. 25 is of particular interest, as its subject is the burning of a Sussex ironmaster Richard Woodman and his wife during the Marian persecution.

Towards the end of the seventeenth century many Dutch patterns were introduced (Fig. 26). These patterns were either of foreign workmanship, or copies from foreign examples. They are smaller and thinner than the majority of earlier backs, and are usually decorated by some historical or allegorical subject, bordered with festoons of fruit and flowers and other detail in the classical taste, carried out in low relief. This class was also used for the backplate of dog-grates.

There are a few Georgian examples (Fig. 27), but not many, as dog-grates and hob-grates, the earlier form of which is termed the 'duck's nest,' were coming into general use about this period.

One of the most conspicuous accessories of the large open fireplaces of dining-rooms and kitchens in the seventeenth and eighteenth centuries is the chimney crane. This was a wrought-iron bracket hung against the back wall of the fireplace, and made to swing to and fro over the hearth. They are known in Scotland as 'sways.' Various sizes and shapes were produced, some quite simple, others very elaborate. The most complex were made with three separate movements. The first enabled the crane to swing in a quarter circle on the vertical heel bar which was stepped in the hearth-stone at the base and fixed at the top by a staple driven into the wall. The second raised and lowered the pot hook attached to the lever, the latter being held in the required position by the studs or catches on the quadrant. The third movement took the whole of the metalwork of the second bodily along the top horizontal bar, running on a wheel; this enabled a utensil hung upon the crane to be moved over any part of the hearth at various levels (Fig. 28).

A very unusual type, having three methods of adjustment, is exhibited in the National Museum of Antiquities, Edinburgh. In this example the hook from which the cauldron or kettle is suspended slides on the top horizontal bar. This, together with the first swinging movement of the whole crane, enables the suspending hook to be adjusted over any part of the hearth. In addition there is a third operation by which the height of the suspending hook may be varied. This is accomplished by turning the vertical crank which by means of a thread at the lower end lifts or lowers the top horizontal bar, the latter being hinged to the top of the vertical bar (Fig. 29). Another crane of a somewhat similar type is shown in Fig. 30, but has a lever and hook in place of the crank and screw for raising and lowering the top arm.

Simple cranes with only the swinging movement are to be met with in many old houses dating from the beginning of the seventeenth century. These are illustrated in Figs 31 and 32, Fig. 31 being a simple Sussex crane ornamented with 'C' scrolls and Fig. 32 a more decorative example from Wales.

In the kitchens of the more important houses where a wide roasting grate was fixed, two of these simple cranes were used; as in the great kitchen at Aston Hall and St. Mary's Guild Hall, Coventry.

With most chimney cranes pot hooks were attached for suspending the cauldrons and cooking utensils. They rank amongst the earlier of domestic metal implements, and are illustrated in many illuminated MSS. Two examples from miniatures are shown in Figs. 33 and 34. Both are from MSS. in the British Museum; Fig. 33 from a thirteenth-century French MS., showing a pot hook with the working principles rather indistinct; it appears to be drawn inverted. The second is clearly represented, and exactly similar to those in use in many parts of the country. Pot hooks, called variously 'cotralls,' jib-crooks,' 'hangers,' and' tramelles,' are frequently mentioned in inventories and household accounts. In a list of Sargeant Keble's goods, dated 1500, there is an item:

'Three pairs of pot hooks and four hanging-irons . . . 10d.'

Among the goods of Dioness Gryme, 1529, there were:

'a peyre of pott hokys and a peyer of pott hangers . . iiijd.'

while in an inventory of the Stationers' Company of 1558, there occurs in the kitchen:

'Item 3 tramelles to hang potts on.'

Existing examples of various types are shown in Figs. 35 to 42. The common type, and the one which corresponds to those illustrated in mediæval MS. is in Fig. 41. 35 and 42 are on the same principle, but more elaborate, and date from the seventeenth century. These three examples were constructed to hang from an iron bar that spanned the chimney, the length being adjusted on the pawl and ratchet principle. The small hooks which are adjusted by hook and eye (Figs. 36 to 39) were made to hang from the chimney cranes. Another method for suspending cauldrons was by a chain of large round links, which could be hooked up or down as required; these are still to be seen in crofters' cottages in Scotland, where they are known as 'jumping ropes' (Fig. 40).

Attached to the bottom of the rachette pot hook, a contrivance known as a 'kettle tilter' was sometimes suspended. This was both ingenious and useful, although it earned for itself the name of 'Idle-back' or 'Lazy-back' because persons using it were supposed to be too idle to take the kettle from off the pot hook. It enables one to pour out the water without making one's hand black.

The working principle of the kettle tilter is in all cases invariably the same; that is to say it is composed of a wrought-iron stem with a loop at the top which is attached to the pot hook, and two hooks with lever handle which is hinged to the lower end of the stem and forms the carrier. The kettle is suspended from the two lower hooks, and is made secure by various methods; some have a spring (Fig. 44), others have lever catches attached to the carrier, either horizontally or vertically, examples are given in Figs. 43 and 45; the latter locks automatically by its own gravity. Another simple and effective arrangement has a stop, or distance piece, welded to the underside of the lever which fits directly over the front hook, making it impossible for the kettle to become dislodged when the lever is depressed.

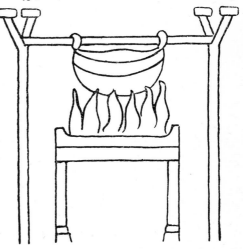

GRATE FROM THE BAYEUX TAPESTRY
11th Century

The earliest grates or braisers used in this country were for out-door cooking, the fire being raised upon an iron frame for convenience. Such an operation is illustrated in the Bayeux tapestry, and is shown here.

The use of grates within the house is of comparatively recent date, except in large establishments where a raised fire was necessary for roasting large joints. With these large roasting grates, which date from the Elizabethan period, the sides were adjustable so that the size of the fire could be proportioned with the size of the joint or carcase.

Of loose grates of wrought iron for use in the fire opening of living-rooms two are shown in Figs. 46 and 47. They both stand on four legs and so dispense with fire-dogs. Fig. 46 is a type belonging to the late sixteenth century, and with this example a fire-back would be necessary. The example in Fig. 47 is on Flemish lines, with fire-bars on all four sides. With this type a small cast-iron fire-back was sometimes fitted to the back.

These grates were the parents of the somewhat elaborate compound dog-grates of the eighteenth century, used in the more important houses (Figs. 48 and 49). They were in many cases constructed to stand in the hearth opening, which had for so long accommodated the fire-dogs. As the name implies, they embodied the dogs and grate and often a small fire-back. They were made in wrought iron, steel, and also cast iron; sometimes brass and bronze frets and mouldings were introduced into the design. This was the last form of unfixed grate used in living-rooms. In the kitchens and parlours of cottages, farmhouses, and inns, a form of portable grate called the 'duck's nest' was largely used in the eighteenth and early nineteenth centuries (Fig. 50) (pot hooks and chimney cranes were still necessary for this variety). This was a low cast-iron grate standing about twelve or fourteen inches from the ground, with a hob at either end, but no oven or boiler; they were suitable for burning both wood and coal. The Scottish equivalent for this form was the 'foreface,' a flat iron grid sometimes decorated by scrollwork and built into brick hobs upon either side of the fire opening.

Trivets are wrought-iron stands to support utensils when off the fire. The usual type has three legs attached to a circular plate or ring with a strengthening stretcher half-way down the legs. This type is shown in Figs. 51 and 52. 51 has a top plate perforated with the date 1692; Fig. 52 dates from the end of the eighteenth century and is of a stock pattern.

The 'cat' is another form of eighteenth-century trivet or plate stand, being made up of six spokes springing from a central body, three at the top and three at the bottom; it could be used either way up, the three lower spokes forming the feet and the three upper supporting the plate (Figs. 53 and 54).

Four-legged trivets were made for two purposes—firstly as stands for the dripping pan under the bottle jacks or dangle spits, which are illustrated in Figs. 55 and 56, and generally as muffin or kettle stands for the parlour, in which case they were called 'footmen.' This type is shown in Figs. 57 and 58.

During the second half of the eighteenth century a form of trivet was made to be hung from the fire-bars. There are two varieties, those with legs, which enabled them to be used as standing trivets (Figs. 59

to 62), and those that could only be attached to the fire-bars (Figs. 63 to 67). Of the first type, Figs. 60 and 61 are of wrought iron, 61 being a stock design made in large quantities. The other two shown in Figs. 59 and 62 have cast brass perforated top plates fixed to wrought-iron frames. This type was a common article of hearth furniture in the better class living-rooms of the period.

The second type of fire-bar trivet, shown in Figs. 63 and 64, are of wrought iron and hang on the near side of the fire, in the usual way; 66, also of wrought iron, is less common, as it is made to support a vessel over the fire. An implement that performs a similar service is the cran, shown in Fig. 67. This is an open wrought-iron frame that fits over the fire, the two short fork feet engaging the top bar of the grate. It is of Scottish origin, and dates from the eighteenth century.

The other small example shown in Fig. 65 is a cast-brass fender trivet, of a type made in large quantities in Birmingham during the last quarter of the eighteenth century. These trivets are suspended from the top rail of the fender as muffin and kettle stands.

An implement used on the cottage down-hearths of the seventeenth and eighteenth centuries is the baking iron (Figs. 70 to 72). They supported a small cast-iron cooking pot, which was pushed among the live embers and so used as an oven for baking bread and cakes. Short-legged trivets were also used for the same purpose, and are shown in Figs. 71 and 72.

Fire implements such as tongs, shovels, and fire-forks are mentioned in numerous manuscripts and household inventories dating from the fifteenth century.

Of the early shovel there are no mediæval examples, but they were probably similar to the crude eighteenth-century pattern shown in Fig. 73. Types used in the living-rooms at this period are of delicate workmanship, and show Continental influence (Figs. 74 and 75). They all differ from modern examples, inasmuch as the pan is welded to the stem and not riveted.

The common form of tongs prior to the introduction of steel fire-iron sets had straight jaws broadened out and almost circular at the top, working upon a hinge. The handle was square in section, tapering towards the end, which was finished off with a knob or blunt spike. They were made in various sizes ranging from twenty to twenty-seven inches in length. This type was used all over the British Isles in the seventeenth, eighteenth, and early nineteenth centuries; the lines of these tongs are simple, but the great drawback to them is that the hinge is unprotected (Figs. 76 and 77).

The fire-fork was a bar of wrought iron about four feet long, with a handle at one end and a two-pronged fork at the other, some having in addition to the fork a spike at the side (Fig. 79). These were for manipulating logs of wood. Tongs with grips at the end of the jaws, made like a bird's claw, were also used for the same purpose (Fig. 78). These usually had a spring handle and worked on the principle of sugar tongs, as did many of the tongs belonging to the fire-iron sets introduced at the end of the eighteenth century.

In mediæval times and right down to the early part of the nineteenth century it was the custom never if possible to let the fire go out but to keep it burning day after day, year in year out, and tradition maintains that in some houses the fire has burned continuously for considerably over a century. To make up a large fire so that it would need no attention all through the night would be extremely wasteful as regards fuel, besides exposing the inmates of the house to a risk of the place catching alight; so to remedy both these drawbacks, the fire was raked together at bed-time and a cover called a 'curfew' (couvre-feu) was placed over them. This was made in sheet brass or copper, roughly in the form of a quartersphere with the handle at the top; it was placed over the embers and pushed against the back of the hearth, cutting off almost all ventilation. In the morning the 'curfew' would be removed, the dull embers raked apart, and fresh fuel placed upon them; then all that was needed was a moment or two with the bellows or blowing tube.

Although at one time curfews must have been comparatively common, they are now one of the rarest of domestic survivals. An example, dated 1584, unfortunately in a rather dilapidated condition, is preserved in Canterbury Museum, and there are three very fine specimens in brass ornamented by rich repoussé work in the Victoria and Albert Museum. The Brighton Museum is also fortunate enough to have a good example in sheet copper decorated by repoussé ornament (Fig. 80). Another perfect brass specimen belonging to The Hon. Mrs. Vickers is shown in Fig. 82.

The blowing tube shown in Fig. 81 is an iron pipe slightly tapered and used in the same way as a pea-shooter. The small crutch at the lower end rested upon the hearthstone, and allowed the air to escape freely among the embers. This implement has been obsolete in England for a long period, and was never popular. It is, however, still quite common in the humbler dwellings in Flanders. Centrifugal hand blowers were in use where peat fuel was in general use. The two examples below are among the many types in use from the eighteenth century. The upper one is of brass with fan box and handle in mahogany. The lower one is from Ireland and is of brass with exception of the mahogany handle. It bears the owner's name and district, and an engraved Irish harp.

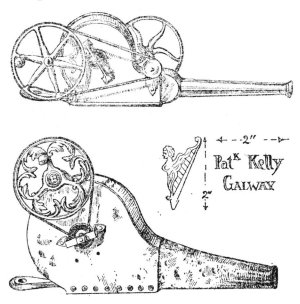

CENTRIFUGAL HAND BLOWERS
*Above: English of brass except mahogany fan box and handle (Author's collection)*
*Below: Irish of brass except mahogany handle (Morris Williams collection)*

Fenders or fend-irons were seldom used with the down-hearth, and only became an essential safety device when the fire was raised, either in a loose or fixed grate. For the down-hearth fend-irons were constructed of a long flat plate set up on edge with the ends returned to keep it upright, or else swept on plan in the form of a long-bow. This was developed by adding a pot stand upon which heavy utensils could be placed. An example of this kind is shown in Fig. 83, which is an eighteenth-century Scots bridal fender, the pot stand being fashioned in the form of two joined hearts; this is the prototype of the modern kitchen fender.

Of the two other examples, Fig. 84 is a simple eighteenth-century cast-iron pattern, and 85 a type of which there are many varieties. It has no return ends, and relies on its swept line for stability.

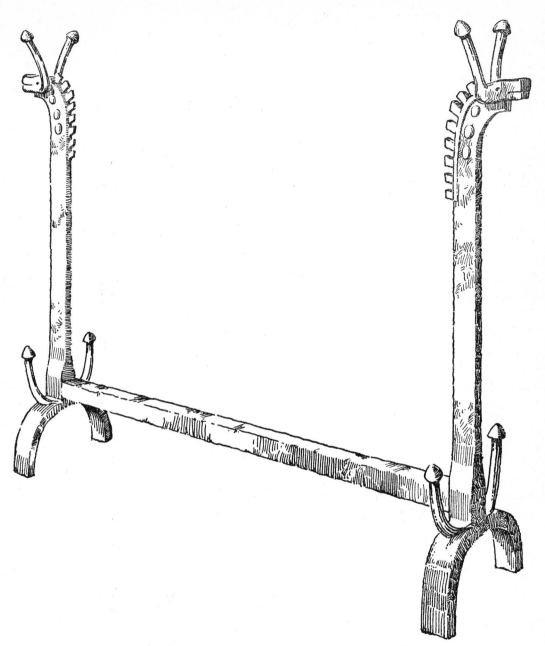

1. WROUGHT-IRON FIRE-DOG, LATE CELTIC

Height 38 ins. *Drawn from the wooden model in the British Museum*

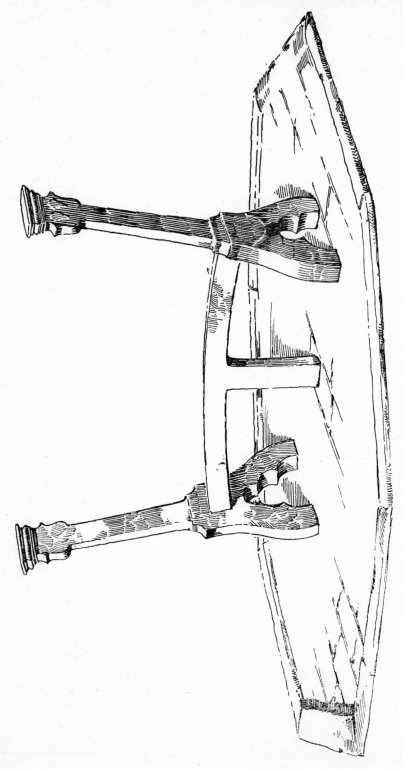

2. CAST-IRON DOUBLE ENDED FIRE-DOG, 16TH CENTURY (MEDIAEVAL TYPE)
Height 3 ft. 8¼ ins. *From Penshurst*

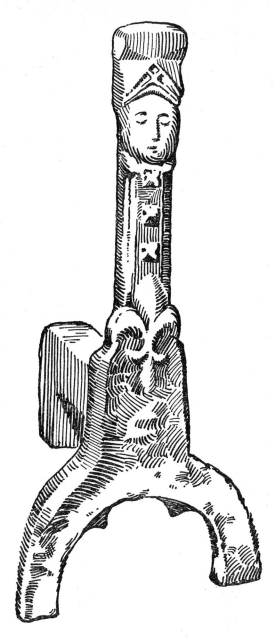

**3. CAST-IRON FIRE-DOG, 16TH CENTURY**
Height 18 ins. *Mr. Charles Wayte's collection*

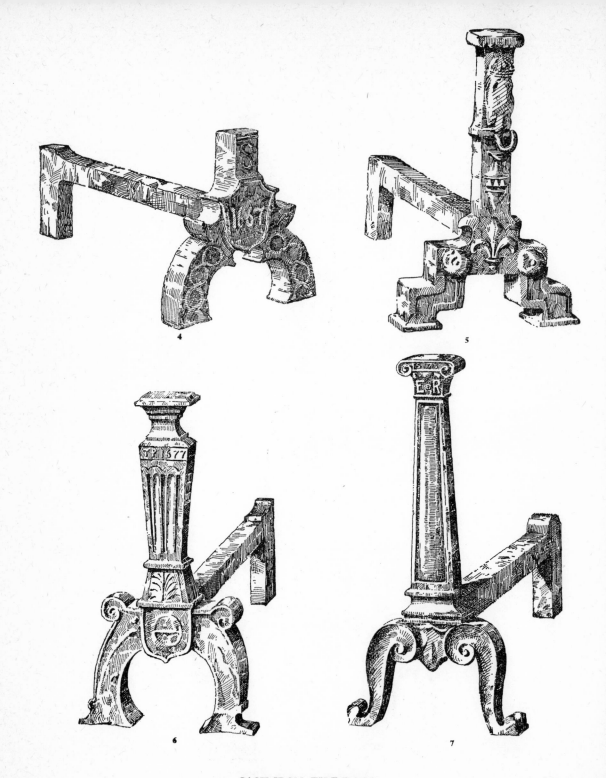

## CAST-IRON FIRE-DOGS

4. DATED 1667. Height 11½ ins. *Victoria & Albert Museum*
5. 17TH CENTURY. Height 15 ins. *Mr. Georges' collection*
6. DATED 1677. Height 18 ins. *Lewes Museum*
7. DATED 1575. Height 22 ins. *Lewes Museum*

8. CAST-IRON FIRE-DOG, DATED 1698

Height 24 ins. *Taken from a drawing in the British Museum by William Twopenny*

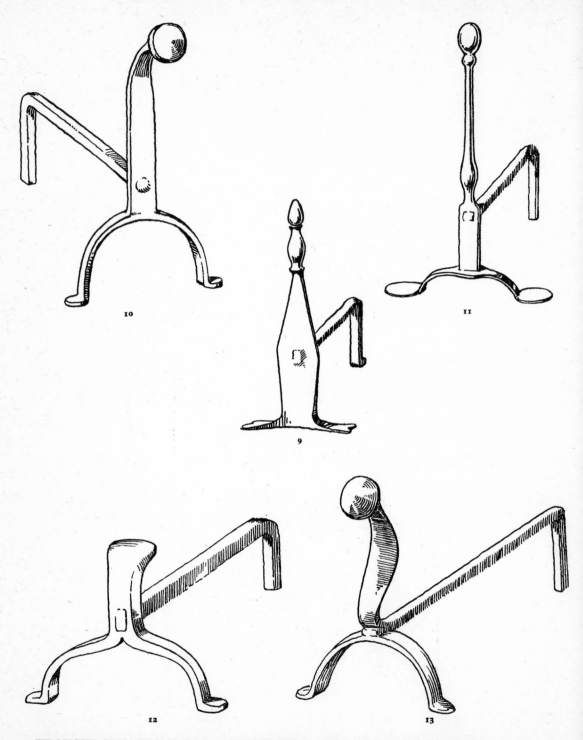

9. WROUGHT-IRON BRAND-DOG, 16TH CENTURY. Height 9¾ ins. *Author's collection*
10. WROUGHT-IRON BRAND-DOG, 18TH CENTURY. Height 12 ins. *Author's collection*
11. WROUGHT-STEEL FIRE-DOG, LATE 18TH CENTURY. Height 11½ ins. *Author's collection*
12, 13. WROUGHT-IRON BRAND-DOGS, 17TH AND 18TH CENTURY TYPES. Height 7 ins. and 9 ins.
*The late L. G. Russell-Davies bequest*

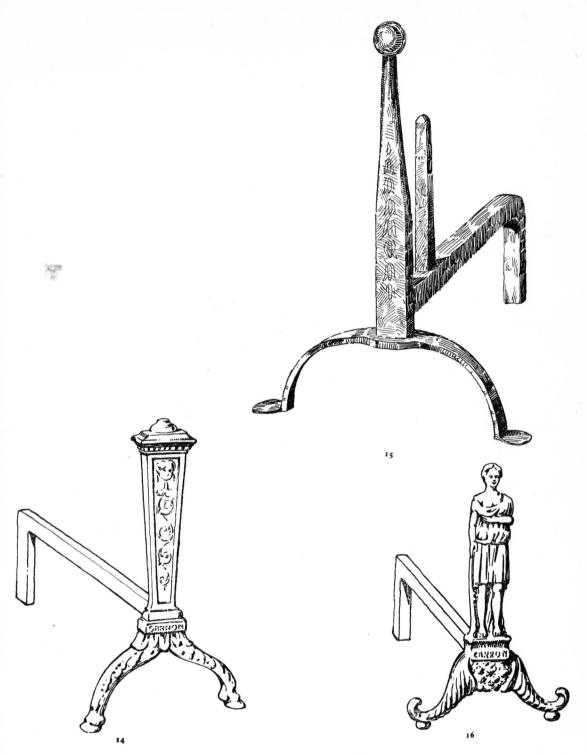

14, 16. CAST-IRON BRAND-DOGS, LATE 18TH CENTURY. Height 13½ ins. and 12 ins.
15. WROUGHT-IRON DOG FOR SUPPORTING GRATE, LATE 18TH CENTURY. Height 19 ins. *Author's collection*

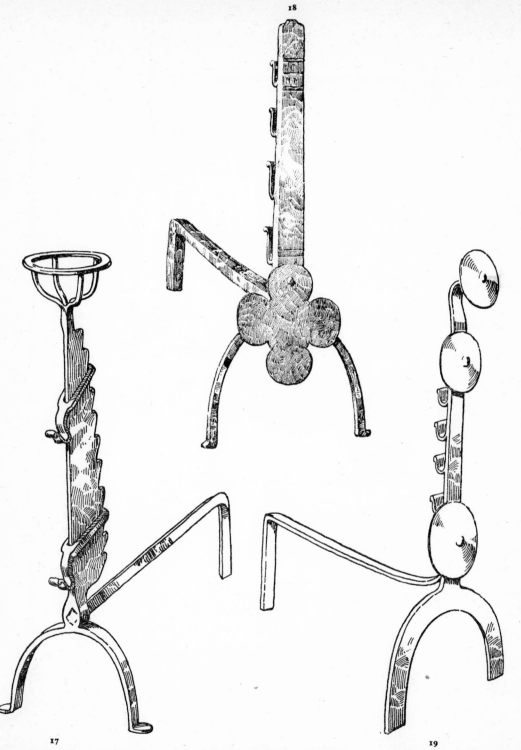

17. WROUGHT-IRON CRESSET SPIT DOG, 17TH CENTURY TYPE. Height 24 ins. *Victoria & Albert Museum*

18. WROUGHT-IRON SPIT DOG, 18TH CENTURY TYPE. Height 22½ ins. *The late L. G. Russell-Davies bequest*

19. WROUGHT-IRON SPIT DOG 17TH CENTURY TYPE. Height 24 ins. *Victoria & Albert Museum*

20. CAST-IRON SUSSEX FIRE-BACK, DATED 1642
*Width 33 ins. Brighton Museum*

21. CAST-IRON SUSSEX FIRE-BACK, DATED 1685
*Width 3 ft. Brighton Museum*

22. CAST-IRON IRISH FIRE-BACK, DATED 1688
*From an old house in Ireland*

23. CAST-IRON FIRE-BACK, DATED 1649
Width 21 ins.  *Mr. Charles Wayte's collection*

24. CAST-IRON SUSSEX FIRE-BACK, DATED 1636
Width 22½ ins. *Hastings Museum*

**25. CAST-IRON SUSSEX FIRE-BACK**
Width 27 ins. *Hastings Museum*

26. CAST-IRON FIRE-BACK, LATE 17TH CENTURY
Width 15¾ ins. *Author's collection*

27. CAST-IRON FIRE-BACK, LATE 18TH CENTURY

Width 21¾ ins. *The late L. G. Russell-Davies bequest*

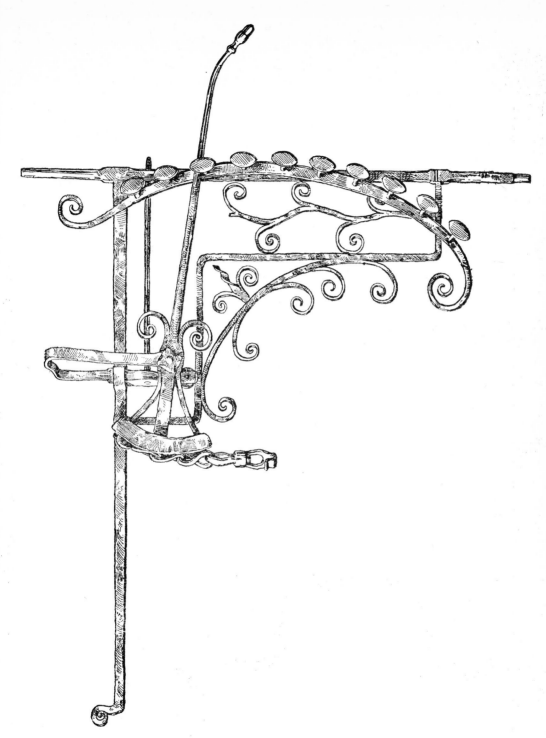

28. WROUGHT-IRON CHIMNEY CRANE WITH THREE MOVEMENTS
Height 33 ins. *Victoria & Albert Museum*

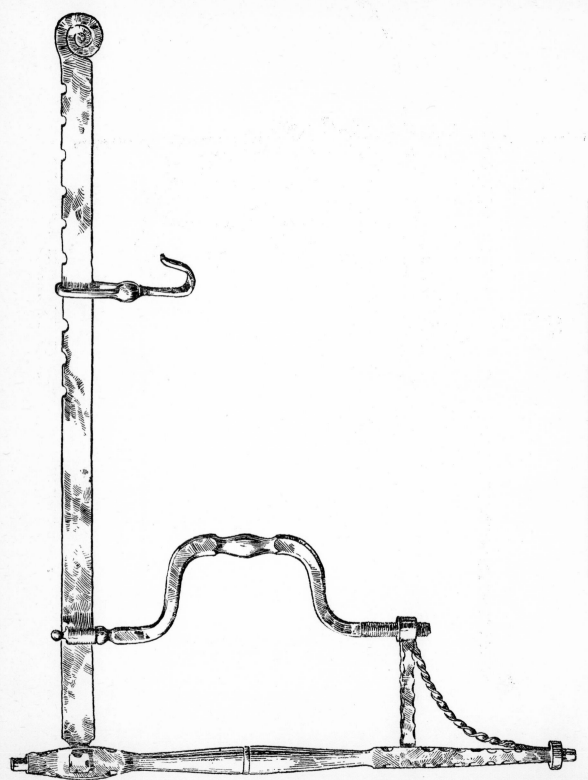

29. WROUGHT-IRON CHIMNEY CRANE WITH TWO MOVEMENTS
Height 26 ins.  *National Museum of Antiquities, Edinburgh*

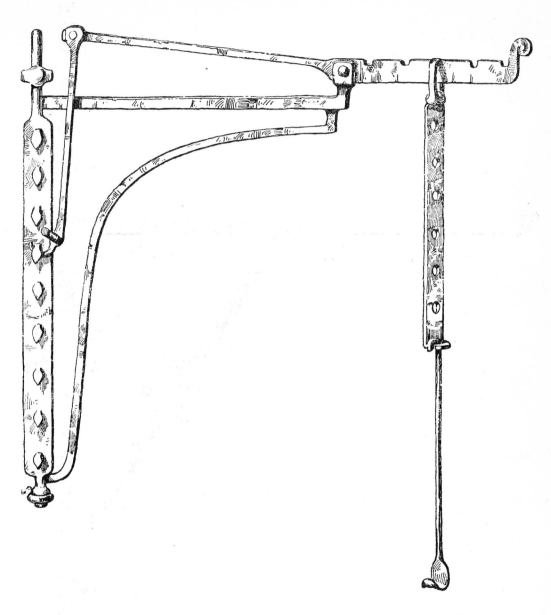

30. WROUGHT-IRON CHIMNEY CRANE WITH TWO MOVEMENTS
Height 30 ins. *From a cottage at Ardingly, Sussex*

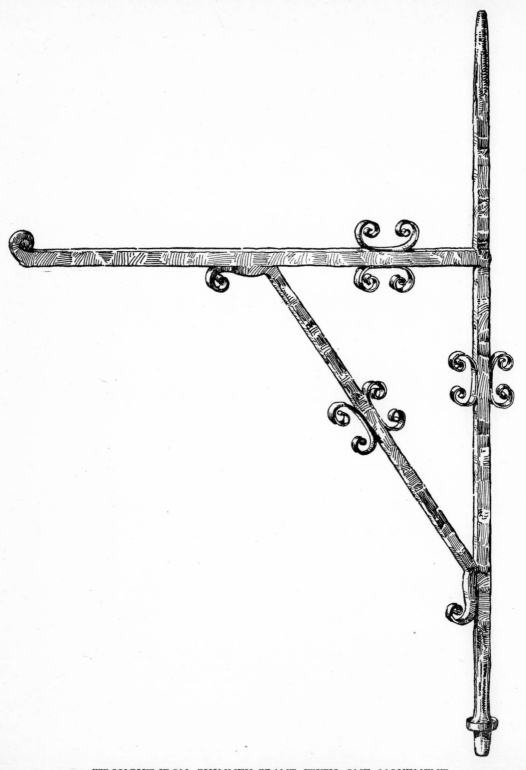

31. WROUGHT-IRON CHIMNEY CRANE WITH ONE MOVEMENT
Height 33 ins. *The late L. G. Russell-Davies bequest*

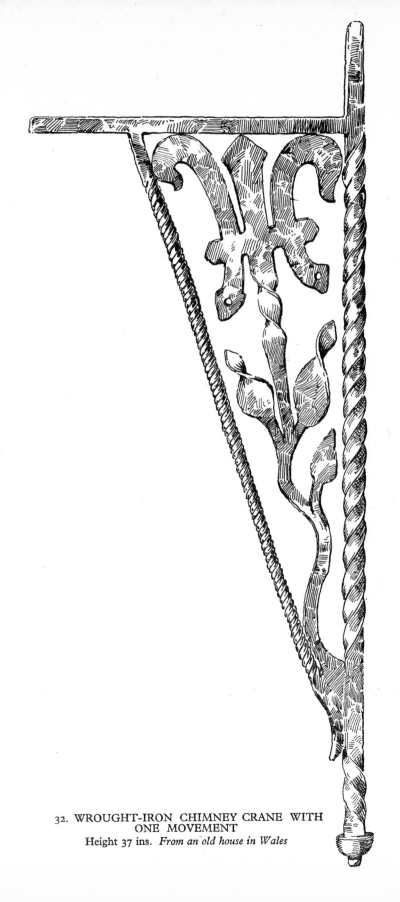

32. WROUGHT-IRON CHIMNEY CRANE WITH
ONE MOVEMENT

Height 37 ins. *From an old house in Wales*

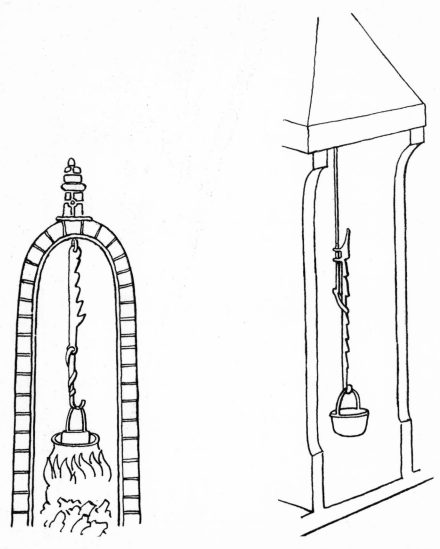

33. POT HOOK AND SKILLET, 13TH CENTURY. (*Add. MS. 18719, f. 253 b.*)
34. POT HOOK AND SKILLET, 15TH CENTURY. (*Harley MSS. 4374, 4375*)

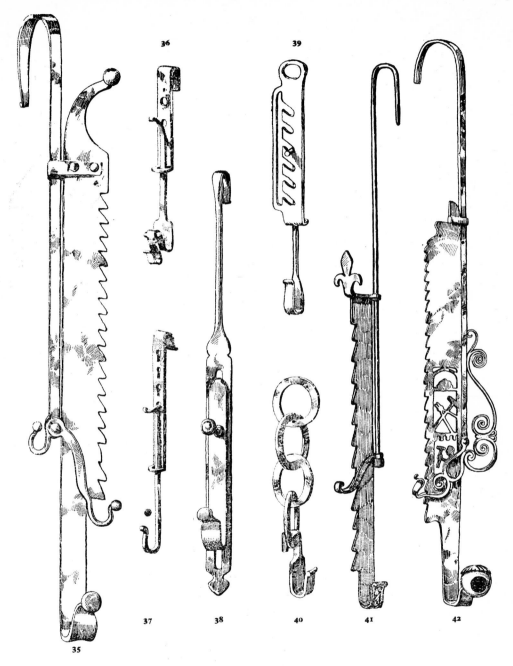

**WROUGHT-IRON POT HOOKS, 16TH, 17TH AND 18TH CENTURY TYPES
DRAWN TO SAME SCALE**
Length of Fig. 35: 3 ft. 7½ ins.

35. *Author's collection*
36. *Mr. R. Turner's collection*
37. *The late L. G. Russell-Davies bequest*
38. *Author's collection*

39. *Hastings Museum*
40. *Mr. J. A. Butti's collection*
41. *The late L. G. Russell-Davies bequest*
42. *Victoria & Albert Museum*

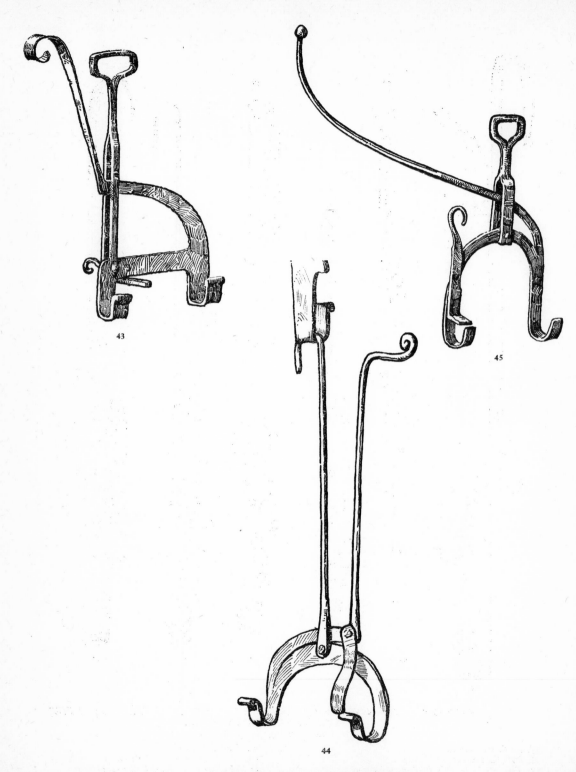

## WROUGHT-IRON KETTLE TILTERS

43. 12 ins. long.  *Author's collection*                    44, 45.  *The late L. G. Russell-Davies bequest*

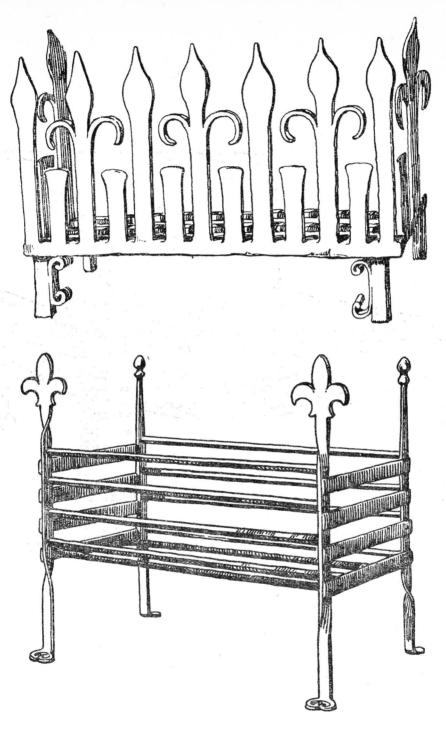

46. WROUGHT-IRON GRATE. *From Haddon Hall*
47. WROUGHT-IRON GRATE. *From Plas Mawr, Wales*

48. DOG-GRATE OF CAST AND WROUGHT IRON, 18TH CENTURY
Width 24½ ins. *From Bowman Bros.*

49. DOG-GRATE OF WROUGHT STEEL AND CAST BACK, LATE 18TH CENTURY
Width 32 ins. *Victoria & Albert Museum*

**50. DUCK'S NEST GRATE OF CAST IRON**
*In the chimney corner of the Crown Inn, Turners Hill, Sussex*

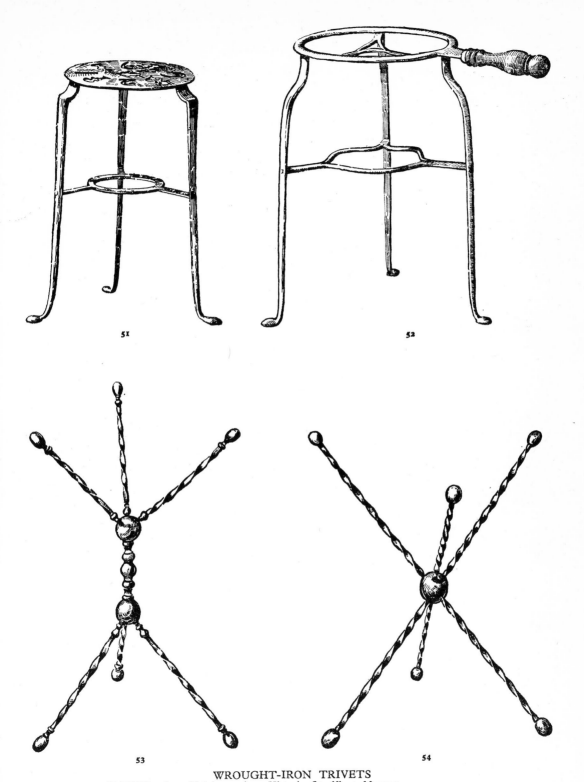

## WROUGHT-IRON TRIVETS

51. DATED 1692. Height 13 ins. *Victoria & Albert Museum*
52. LATE 18TH CENTURY TYPE. Height 15 ins. *Author's collection*
53, 54. 'CATS'. Height 18½ ins. *From the collection of the late Lady Dorothy Neville*

**55, 56. WROUGHT-IRON TRIVETS, EARLY 19TH CENTURY TYPES.** *The late L. G. Russell-Davies bequest*
**57, 58. WROUGHT-IRON TRIVETS, 18TH CENTURY.** *Victoria & Albert Museum*

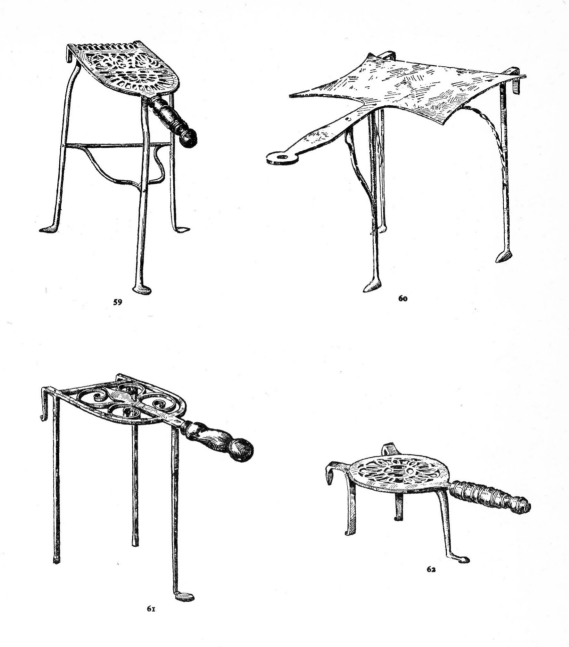

**59**

**60**

**61**

**62**

59, 61. TRIVETS, LATE 18TH CENTURY. *Author's collection*
60. TRIVET, LATE 18TH CENTURY. *Mr. R. Turner's collection*
62. TRIVET, LATE 18TH CENTURY, WITH CAST-BRASS TOP PLATES. *Mr. R. Turner's collection*

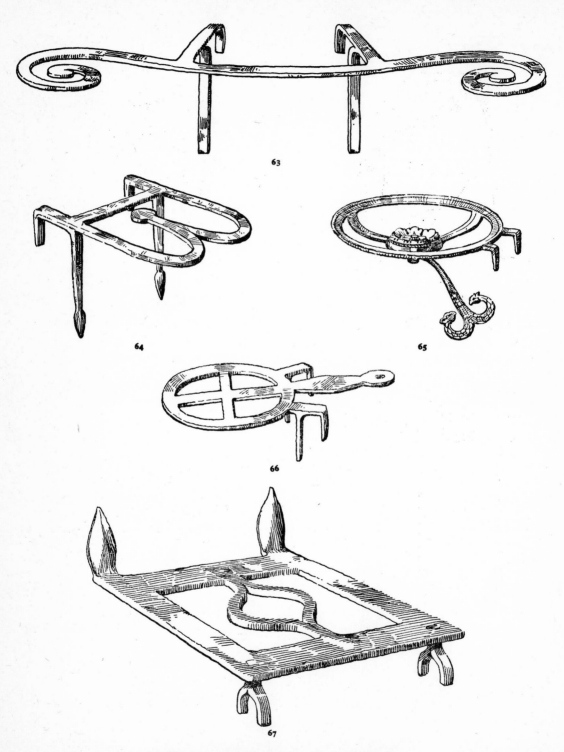

**FIRE-BAR TRIVETS, LATE 18TH CENTURY**

63. *Mr. Oswald Barron's collection*         64–67. *Author's collection*

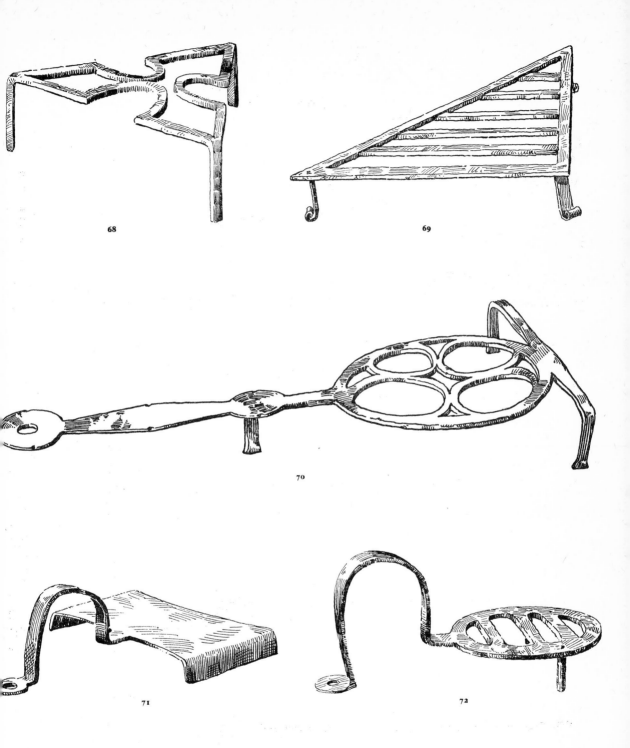

## BAKING IRONS

68, 69, 72. 18TH CENTURY. *Author's collection*
70. 17TH CENTURY. *Mr. Oswald Barron's collection*
71. 17TH CENTURY. *The late L. G. Russell-Davies bequest*

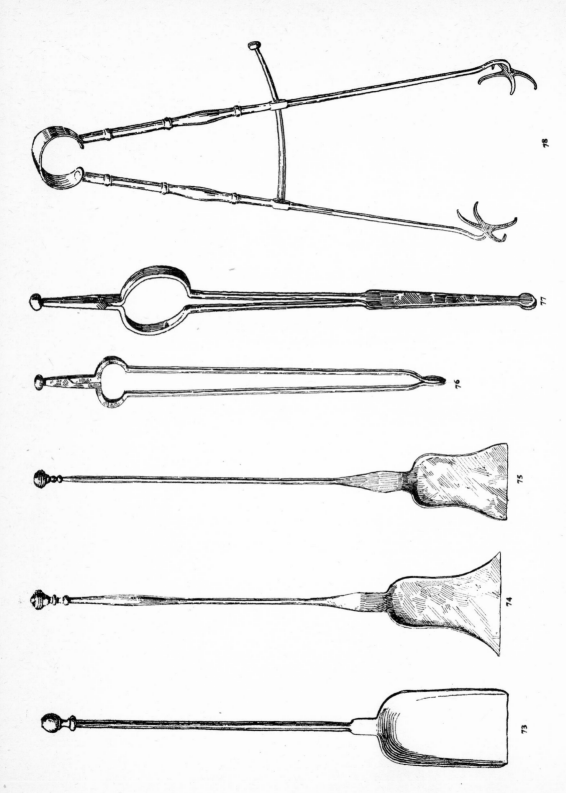

73-75. WROUGHT-IRON SHOVELS, LATE 18TH CENTURY. *Author's collection*
76, 77. WROUGHT-IRON TONGS, 17TH CENTURY. *The late L. G. Russell-Davies bequest*
78. WROUGHT-IRON WOOD TONGS, 18TH CENTURY. *From Sussex*

79. FIRE-FORK, 17TH CENTURY TYPE
80. CURFEW, COPPER REPOUSSÉ, 17TH CENTURY. Width 24 ins. *Brighton Museum*
81. BLOWING TUBE. Length 33 ins. *The late Lady Dorothy Neville's collection*
82. CURFEW, BRASS, 17TH CENTURY. *Hon. Mrs. Vickers' collection*

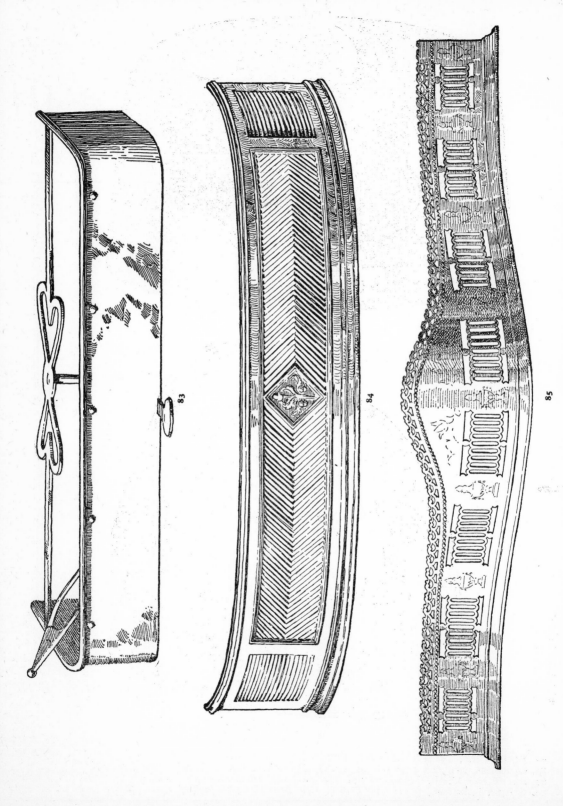

83. WROUGHT-IRON SCOTS BRIDAL FENDER, 18TH CENTURY. *Mr. J. A. Butti's collection*
84. CAST-IRON FENDER, LATE 18TH CENTURY. Length 3 ft. 6 ins. *Geffrye Museum*
85. COPPER FENDER, PERFORATED AND ENGRAVED, LATE 18TH CENTURY. Length 4 ft. *Mr. C. H. F. Walker-Kinderman's collection*

# PART TWO

# THE KITCHEN

CAST AND ENGRAVED BRASS TRIVET
*similar to the engraving on the spit driving gear shown in Fig. 94*

PART TWO

# THE KITCHEN

FROM EARLY HISTORICAL TIMES metal implements have been used in these islands for the preparation of food. Saxons and Normans were both fairly well supplied, but it was not until the twelfth and thirteenth centuries that baronial kitchens were fully equipped and the cooking and serving of food became one of the arts.

With the great expansion of commercial industry in the late Middle Ages, and the consequent growth of the yeoman and trading classes, a great increase took place in the manufacture of cooking utensils.

In Saxon times meat was roasted on spits or skewers of hazel wood, and turned by hand in front of a large fire in the open. Joints, birds, and game of all sorts and sizes were cooked in this way. In the mediæval period meat spits or broches of iron were generally turned by hand, in which case one end of the spit was made in the form of a handle. The work of turning the spits was sometimes performed by a boy especially appointed for the task (Fig. 86).

The popularity of roasting by spits is proved by the numerous references to them in household accounts and inventories. In an Inventory of the Crown Jewels made in the third year of Edward III there occurs:

'1 patella ferri pro friatura Broch' ferri magni 2 turnar' ferri,'

while among Sargeant Keble's goods in 1500 were the following:

'Two great round broches      6s.
Two bird broches      1s.
Little round broche      1s. 8d.'

Wrought-iron spits were made in various forms, the most common being the straight spit with a spike at one end and a grooved or double flanged driving wheel at the other (Figs. 87 and 88), except in the case of hand-turned spits where a handle took the place of the wheel. The older examples are fitted with wheels made of hard wood fixed to the shaft by an iron cotter pin (87); but the more recent ones have metal wheels. The shaft is flat in the middle, becoming round at the ends, thus enabling them to turn smoothly upon the spit dogs. A double pronged fork slides freely up and down the shaft, being made fast by means of a thumbscrew; this secures the joint in the right position, forcing it to revolve with the spit. Their weight and size varied according to their use, those for game being much lighter than those for joints; bird spits upon which larks and other small birds were roasted were only about three feet long and when required were lashed on to a long game-spit. Spits, when out of use, usually hung in a rack over the mantelshelf.

A later and altogether different type is the basket spit. This has the advantage that the joint is not pierced in any way, but revolves inside an iron cage, the sides of which take off by unscrewing two fly nuts (Fig. 89).

When in use spits usually revolved on spit dogs, examples of which have been shown in Part I (Figs. 17-19).

Alternative appliances are the cob irons shown in Figs. 90 to 92. These were used in pairs one each side of the hearth opening.

The earliest machine for turning spits is the dog and drum, a principle which is of Classic origin. This method obtained for many centuries as is shown in Fig. 93, which is from a drawing by Rowlandson executed whilst touring in North Wales in 1798. This shows a dog running up the inner surface of a drum, the power being transmitted to the spit by a chain drive.

Doctor Caius, founder of Caius College, Cambridge, an authority on dogs, writing about the middle of the seventeenth century says: 'There is comprehended under the curs of the coarsest kind a certain dog in kitchen service excellent. For when any meat is to be roasted, they go into a wheel, which they turning about with the weight of their bodies, so diligently look to their business, that no drudge nor scullion can do the feat more cunningly, whom the popular sort hereupon term turnspits.'

An eighteenth-century writer, speaking of these dogs, describes them as 'long-bodied, crook-legged, and ugly dogs, with a suspicious, unhappy look about them, as if they were weary of the task they had to do, and expected every moment to be seized upon to perform it.'

The weight-driven spit jack came into use towards the end of the

22

sixteenth century, and lasted until spits became obsolete. An early reference occurs in an Inventory of Furniture, etc., in a Bishopsgate Street tavern, dated 1612:

'Item, one Jack, with a waighte                                        10s.'

This machine worked on much the same principle as the weight-clock, the weight being wound up on a drum having at one end the wooden driving wheels which are connected to the spit by a leather belt or chain. The drum is geared up through spur and worm gear to a fly-wheel, which enables the spit to be turned very slowly at a uniform speed and to overcome any extra resistance caused by the unequal balance of the joint upon the spit. These jacks were made in wrought iron as a rule although there are some examples with front plates and wheels of the worm gear of brass: the principle upon which they work is the same in all cases, although the arrangement of the gearing varies slightly. These machines are shown in Figs. 94 to 98. 94, dated 1670, has an engraved brass front plate depicting Atlas supporting the globe; 95 is of wrought iron, ornamented with Fleur-de-lis and incised lines and dated 1680. Of the other two, 96 is the standard wrought-iron eighteenth-century type, and 97 is of the same period, but has the weight attached to a continuous chain that was drawn up from time to time. The small illustration (Fig. 98) is taken from the *Journal* of Timothy Burrell, in which occurs an entry under the date of 1692:

'26th March. Paid Green for a new jack £1.10.6 and he is to keep the wheels and the pulley in good order for 6d. a year.'

Against the entry is this small sketch, in very crude perspective, showing the jack with weighted flier.

Another arrangement for turning spits is the smoke jack, which still exists in many eighteenth-century houses. This derives its power from the upward rush of hot air from the fire revolving a paddle or rotor in the chimney: the latter turned the wooden driving wheels which projected from the wall over the fireplace. The one illustrated is from Falmer Court, Sussex, and Fig. 99 shows the rotor connected to a shaft running at right angles by a worm gear which is enclosed in an iron box; the sides are removed in the sketch, revealing the large brass wheel which turns in an oil bath. This oil bath also accommodates the bottom bearing of the rotor spindle; the top bearing is provided with a grease cup which is protected from falling soot by a flat iron covering. The shaft upon which the wooden driving wheels are fixed is supported by an iron bar, upon the outer extremity of which is a grease cup enclosing a roller bearing. In many of the larger early nineteenth-century kitchens these smoke jacks were made on more elaborate lines, the rotor being connected to a long horizontal shaft above the fireplace, at each end of which were wooden or brass driving wheels for the spits. At intervals along the shaft were suspended the 'dangle spits;' these by means of bevel wheels revolved vertically in front of the fire. This device would appear obsolete at the beginning of the nineteenth century, according to Count Romford, quoted in Loudon's *Encyclopædia of Architecture* (1833). The following quotation gives the Count's opinion of smoke jacks: 'To complete the machinery of an ordinary British kitchen range, which seems to be calculated for the express purpose of devouring fuel, a smoke jack is generally placed in the chimney.' No human invention, Count Romford adds, ever came to his knowledge that was so absurd as this; it would not be difficult to prove, he says, 'that much less than one thousandth part of the fuel that is necessary to be burned in an open chimney fireplace, in order to cause a smoke jack to turn a loaded spit, would be sufficient to make the spit go round, were the force evolved from the combustion of the fuel, if it were properly directed through the medium of a steam-engine.' The article goes on to state that 'besides this waste of fuel and of power, smoke jacks require a large fire when it would not otherwise be wanted, by the necessity which they create for a great current of air up the chimney, to prevent it from smoking. This also increases the current of cold air from the doors and windows to the fireplace; and thus, while the side of the cook next the fire is burned the other is chilled. A jack moved by a weight or spring, if roasting must still be performed by the barbarous practice of turning meat on a spit before an open fire, is much preferable; and the trouble of winding it up, which is a general argument against it, is much less than that of burning coal to feed the immense fire that is required to cause a common smoke jack to move.'

A simple form of dangle spit, the immediate forerunner of the bottle jack, had an adjustable hook or group of hooks suspended by a cord, the winding and unwinding of which provided the rotary movement which was assisted by two weighted flyers at the top of the metal stem (Fig. 100).

Spring-driven jacks were the last of the mechanical devices used for turning meat before an open fire. Of the two illustrated, Fig. 101 derives its power from a spring concealed within a drum and is wound up by a handle projecting from the face. This machine occupied a position above one end of the mantelshelf. As in the majority of spring-driven jacks, there is no attempt at ornament. The last device is the clock-work bottle jack (102). This either hung in a Dutch oven, or was suspended from a jack rack screwed or clamped above the fireplace: the latter implements are shown in Figs. 103 to 107.

From the earliest historical times cauldrons have been among the most important articles of the household. The prototype is the late Bronze Age specimen (Fig. 108). This is constructed of six sheets of hammered bronze and suspended by two ring handles. The eighth-century Saxon type (Fig. 109) is carried in the same way, also the Norman example from the Bayeux Tapestry (page 13, Part I). The earlier mediæval boiling vessels are of cast bronze, standing on three long legs and lifted by two lug handles springing from the top rim. This type (Figs. 111 and 112) is similar to that illustrated in a fourteenth-century MS. in the British Museum (Fig. 110 ). The later mediæval variety is similar, but with much shorter legs. A small fifteenth-century bronze water vessel showing Flemish influence (Fig. 116) is suspended by an iron handle, the liquid being drawn off through either of the two spouts. Cast-iron cauldrons of this and the following century (Fig. 113 to 115) are similar in form to the bronze vessels. As the cast-iron industry expanded they were made in large quantities for farm-houses and cottage use, and continued to be an indispensable utensil in all kitchens with down-hearths and open grates. Except in the larger houses, meat was more often boiled than roasted, as the former method needed much less fuel and attention. A common method among cottagers was to hang the various kinds of vegetables and meat round the inside of the pot in nets. Iron cauldrons were also used as ovens for baking cakes or game, either inverted with the ashes heaped around or standing upon the hearth with the top closed by an iron plate or lid. The former method made 'upset' and the latter 'pot-oven-bread.'

The mediæval equivalent to the modern saucepan was the skillet, posnet, or pipkin (Fig. 120). This was a small cast-bronze cauldron in miniature, with a stem handle attached to the rim. Being a down-hearth utensil, it was necessary that it should have legs to set it above the embers. In the Roll of Expenses of Edward I at Rhuddlan Castle, made in 1281 and 1282, there is an entry:

'For a Posnet bought for the Lady Elizabeth, the King's
daughter                                                os. 6d.'

A miniature in a fourteenth-century MS. at the British Museum illustrates a contemporary skillet.

14TH-CENTURY SKILLET AND SPOON (*MS. Reg. 10 E. IV*)

Sixteenth- and seventeenth-century cast-bronze skillets were no longer modelled on the lines of cauldrons, the opening being greater than the base and the bottom almost flat. During this period three kinds were in use, the most common being three-legged, with long straight tapered handle often decorated or bearing an inscription or maker's name (Figs. 121, 123, and 124). The name on one of the handles is that of Thomas Palmar, who was the son of John Palmar, both Kent bell founders of the early seventeenth century.

The second type was supported by a three-legged wrought-iron stand, a brandreth with long handle welded to the top ring (122); the third, and least common, was a cast or sheet-brass vessel suspended by an iron loop handle from a pot hook, in a similar manner to the bronze pot (Fig. 116 and Figs. 33 and 34).

Although there is no risk in using a properly tinned copper vessel, there seems to have been, towards the end of the eighteenth and beginning of the nineteenth century, a campaign against the employment of bell-metal, copper, and brass utensils. A pamphlet was

26

published in 1755 entitled 'Serious reflections attending the use of copper vessels.' It stated that 'the great frequency of palsies, apoplexies, madness, and all the frightful train of nervous disorders which suddenly attack us without our being able to account for the cause or which gradually weaken our vital faculties are the pernicious effects of this poisonous matter taken into the body insensibly with our vittles and thereby intermixed with our blood and juices.'

Many cookery books had a great deal to say about the evil consequences 'of eating food dressed in copper vessels, not sufficiently cleaned from rust,' and recount tragedies which have occurred from time to time owing to cooks sending food to table which had been kept from the preceding day in copper vessels badly tinned. In one of these articles entitled 'Considerations on culinary poisons,' which appears at the end of an eighteenth-century cookery book, it is asserted that 'on this account the Senate of Sweden, about the year 1753, prohibited copper vessels and ordered that no vessels except such as were made of iron should be used in their fleets and armies.'

Bronze ewers and flagons were used only in the great mediæval establishments. Conspicuous among this class of work are two flagons, one in the British Museum (Fig. 128), and the other of very similar design though smaller, in the Victoria and Albert Museum. This is a flagon for holding hot spiced wine and other drinks from an old manor house in Norfolk. It is of bell-metal embossed with the Royal Arms of England (ancient), repeated several times. The inscription runs: 'Goddis [God's] Grace be in this place. Amen. Stone uttir [Stand away] From the Fyre [fire] and lat [let] oujust [one just] come here [near].'

The example in the British Museum is complete with octagonal lid, and has sixteen animals figured upon it in low relief. The inscriptions upon this vessel are:

> 'He that will not spare when he may
> He shall not spend when he would.'
> 'Deem the best in every doubt
> Till the truth be tried out.'

It is decorated with the arms of England with the badge of Richard II, and was brought home to England from Ashanti by the British expedition of 1896.

Another class of bronze work, indispensable in the large establishments of the early mediæval period, was the acquamanile or ewer

(Figs 126 and 127). As forks had not been introduced, all food was taken in the hand and between each course it was the custom to wash.

This practice is illustrated in a MS. of the fourteenth century, which shows a servant carrying a ewer and basin. A similar ewer or

14TH-CENTURY EWER AND BASIN
(MS. Reg. 10 E. IV)

SEAL OF
SANDRE DE GLOUCESTER
14th Century

lavapot forms part of the design of the seal of Sandre de Gloucetie a fourteenth-century brass founder established at Gloucester. The arms of the Founders Company of London include a pot of the same kind between two pricket candlesticks.

The bronze jug (Fig. 125) is of fifteenth-century type from Edinburgh, and was discovered whilst digging the foundations of South Bridge.

Eighteenth- and early nineteenth-century utensils used for heating water or ale are shown in Figs. 129 to 132. The kettle (129) is of sheet copper with wrought-iron handle, the long top loop being made to engage in the two bottom hooks of a kettle tilter. Fig. 130 was used upon a trivet or footman with the flat back placed close to the fire-bars: it is of sheet copper. Fig. 132 is similar, but is constructed to hang from the fire-bar by a hook at the back.

Ale warmers were in general use during the Georgian period, the most common type being a conical vessel that was driven into the heart of the fire in a vertical position. Another type known as a 'boot' which, could be used upon a down-hearth, had a projection at the side that was thrust into the fire (Fig. 131).

It is not possible to give the date when mortars were first used in this country, but they certainly formed part of the equipment of great mediæval kitchens. A richly-decorated specimen, weighing seventy-six pounds and dated 1308, is in the Yorkshire Philosophical Society's Museum at York. It was made by Willelmus de Touthorp for the Infirmary of the Abbey of St. Mary. When the art of casting iron became a living industry, mortars were made in this metal; but bronze and later brass continued to be the common metal until they passed out of general domestic use. Jacobean examples in bronze retained the mediæval form. Such a one is in the Victoria and Albert Museum (Fig. 133): it is inscribed in Lombardic lettering:

'William Carter made me for George Beere'

followed by the maker's mark and the date 1615.

A cast-iron example of the same period, Fig. 134, shows Renaissance influence; Figs. 135 and 136 are the common type of cast eighteenth-century iron mortar.

A pestle of this period (137) is of bell-metal, and like most of the early examples, single-ended.

In mediæval kitchens mortars were used in the same way as the modern pastry bowl, and also for powdering such things as ginger, spices, almonds, candy, etc.: they continued to be employed for the latter purpose until these various ingredients were supplied in powdered form.

Gridirons have changed little in form during the long period of their usefulness. The mediæval examples had an extra long handle, as it was necessary to stand back from the fire owing to the great heat. The most usual seventeenth- and eighteenth-century type had a circular grid with flat handle. They were either held over the fire or placed upon a brandreth or baking iron, according to the size of the fire. Another form of this period has a four-sided grid supported upon three legs some three or four inches from the ground. The grid is composed of seven bars, three of which are ornamented by an open-work heart; the handle is flattened out in the centre in the form of a heart, upon which is incised the initials I. C. N. (Fig. 139). A similar gridiron of later date is constructed to rest upon the top bar of a grate.

Made with four short feet, it has the two nearest the handle forked like a cran: the bars of the grid are channelled and drain into a common trough, from which the gravy is poured through a spout at one side (Fig. 138).

Wrought-iron toasters have been used with every kind of hearth and grate, and consequently exist in a number of different forms. The earliest type is represented by the low squat examples used on a down-hearth; of these, there are two kinds, one for toasting bread (Fig. 143) and the other meat (142). They both stand upon three short feet, the former having a contrivance similar to a toast-rack which revolves, enabling both sides to be turned to the fire without removing the bread, and the latter being provided with a fork, under which is a tray for the dripping. The two-pronged fork is made to hinge back, so that the meat can be removed or turned more easily.

With the advent of the grate, two kinds of toasters were made—those supported from the fire bar, and those standing upon three legs of sufficient height to bring the prongs in line with the fire. Of the former, 144 is for bacon and 145 for bread. In both cases the carrier revolves and slides to and fro, so enabling the food to be taken off without unshipping the toaster. Another type is peculiar to Scotland (140 and 141) used for baking flat scones or bannocks, which were supported in a vertical position by the ornamental frame-work.

The most common type of standard toaster for use in front of a grate or raised hearth has the prongs fitted to a slide which slides upon the upright stem and is held in position by a friction spring; some have a plate carrier fitted underneath which slides independently of the prongs, such a device being necessary when meat was cooked so as to catch the dripping (Fig. 146). Others were constructed with the toasting fork supported from a three-legged trivet (147), the fork being adjustable both in height and extension.

Wafer irons are wrought-iron implements fashioned like black-smiths' tongs, but with the jaws made of two flat discs four to five inches in diameter, the inner surface being covered with incised ornament (Figs. 148 and 149). They were used in making wafer bread for the Mass and other religious ceremonies, but their use was not entirely ecclesiastical. In an apprizement of goods and chattels of Stephen de Northerne, 1358, there occurs 'One pair of irons for the Eucharist,' and in a fifteenth-century cookery book there is the following recipe, which shows that these irons were in common secular use.

'Waffres [wafers]—Take the womb [stomach] of a luce [full grown pike] and sethe here wyl and do it on a mortar and tender chese thereto, grynde them togethir; then take flour and white of eyroun and beat together, then take sugar and pouder of gyngere and do all together and look that the eyroun be hot and lay thereon a thin paste and then make thin waffrys and so on.'

This recipe is given in *Two Fifteenth-Century Cookery Books*, the editor translating the word 'eyroun' as egg. This word occurs again and to make sense it must be read as also meaning iron.

In the Churchwardens' Accounts of St. Mary Redcliffe, Bristol, there is an entry:

'To a pair of wafer Irons                                    iijs iijd.'

This form of bread was used at Westminster Abbey until 1643. Wafers were also made on the Mid-Sunday in Lent, when it was the custom in many parts for young people to visit their mothers, taking with them some of these cakes.

In the *History and Antiquities of Claybrook*, 1791, there occurs the following passage:

'At Leckford near Stockbridge Hants. this ie. Mothering Sunday is called Wafering Sunday from the wafer-cakes impressed with an iron bearing an impression like a seal, offered by young people to their mothers on this occasion. The iron has two stamps; three locked hearts surmounted by a cross enclosed within a circle, and an anchor with foliated ornaments on either side. Two or three of these utensils, which were made red-hot over a charcoal fire, seemed to suffice for the village which employs a person called a waferer to do the work.'

Wafer tongs continued to be used for domestic purposes until the early nineteenth century as the following recipe, taken from a cookery book of that period, shows:

'Dry the flour well which you intend to use, mix a little pounded sugar and finely pounded mace with it; then make it into a thick batter with cream; butter the wafer irons, let them be hot; put a teaspoonful of batter into them, so bake them carefully, and roll them off the iron with a stick.'

Chestnut roasters of the eighteenth century and later were made with a sheet iron cylindrical box about seven inches wide by three inches deep, having the lid and side perforated. Attached to the side is a wrought-iron handle, two feet long with wood hand-piece. To enable the box to be opened conveniently without burning or soiling the hands, it has a second handle attached to the lid, which, when the box is shut, lies upon and fastens to the longer handle, to which it is made fast by an iron button about half-way down the stem (Fig. 150).

These roasters were not made in cast brass, but the pattern has been reproduced in large quantities in this metal during the last few years, on a rather smaller though more elaborate scale.

Another utensil of this period is the coffee roaster (Fig. 151). The sheet iron container is fitted with a sliding door, and inside are fixed two fins of metal which cause the coffee to be mixed and so equally roasted.

During the seventeenth century the warming-pan was an article of common domestic use. In an Inventory of Furniture, etc., of a Tavern in Bishopgate Street, dated 1612, there is an item, 'One warmynge-panne,' priced at three shillings, and in 1656 the Reverend Giles More, in his Journal, mentions having bought one from 'Johnson at the shop in Grace Church Street, Brasier' for seven shillings and sixpence.

The more expensive type have wrought-iron handles ornamented with brass mouldings, the lid of the pan being richly perforated (Fig. 152). A cheaper variety, made in large quantities during the eighteenth century, had a turned wood handle with a pan of copper or brass decorated by incised ornament. The lids were usually perforated to allow the heat to escape more easily from the hot cinders. The fumes were liable to soil the bed linen during the process of warming; this fact no doubt occasioned the making of the hot-water pan, an article which only differs from the later type of warming-pan inasmuch as it has a round copper bottle in place of the ember pan.

MEDIÆVAL BAKEHOUSE  (*MS. Canon. lit. 99, Bodleian*)

32

A variety of implements were made in connection with the baking of bread.

Throughout the Middle Ages bread was supplied in the towns by men whose sole business was to make it. Their method of baking was the same as that employed in most farmhouses during the eighteenth and early nineteenth centuries, namely, heating a brick or stone oven by burning a number of faggots within the oven itself, raking out the ashes and then inserting the batch, which would be baked by the heat stored up in the masonry. The hot embers were withdrawn by an iron spade-like implement called a slice (Fig. 154).

The salamander was used by bakers and others for browning pastry, mashed potatoes, etc.; it was made of a long bar of wrought iron which formed a handle, sometimes with a wooden covering, at the end of which is either a square or circular plate about five or six inches wide and three-quarters of an inch thick. It was placed in the fire until red-hot, then held a short distance from the crust which was quickly scorched by the radiated heat (Fig. 155 and 156). Some examples have short legs fixed to the stem which support the disc about six inches from the ground; these are the older type and were used with the down-hearth (158).

The potato rake (157) was a fairly common down-hearth implement of the eighteenth and nineteenth centuries.

Girdle plates (Fig. 159 and 160) were employed for baking oatbread and small cakes and are still largely used in Scotland and the north of England in houses where the open fire exists. In small houses and cottages in Scotland the girdle plate often stood in a perpendicular position at the back of the grate and acted as a fire-back, where it could easily be pulled down over the fire when required. It was sometimes supported by an iron cran (described on page 15) which rested upon the front bar of the grate. When employed with the down-hearth, they stood upon a brandreth (161) or baking iron, unless they were provided with a half-hoop handle for attaching to the pot hook. A similar implement is the brander (164). This was suspended over an open fire and used for making brander bannocks, flat circular loaves of oatmeal and water. This form of bread was turned by a bread spade (162).

Peculiar to the open fire is the long-handled frying-pan, with wrought-iron handle which, in some examples, is fully three feet long, thus allowing the user to stand well away from the fire. Frying-pans were also made with half-hoop handle and swivel ring at the top for suspending from a pot hook (Fig. 163).

Eighteenth-century skimmers were of two types, the most common having a long iron handle attached to a circular pan of brass, copper, or tinned iron, the surface being perforated with small round holes (Figs. 165 and 166). The second type (170), known as a 'flit,' is provided with a small ring handle, and was used for taking the cream from milk. The fish slice (167) is of cast brass, and was a common type in seventeenth- and eighteenth-century kitchens.

Of the two ladles (168 and 169), the former is of cast brass and was for basting and skimming. This type has been much reproduced of recent years for decorative purposes. The latter, having a deep copper pan and long iron handle, is for ladling only. A fourteenth-century cookery spoon or ladle is shown on page 26.

Forks were made for two purposes, toasting and handling food. Of the former the most primitive is not strictly speaking a fork, as it is composed of a two-pronged rack socketed to the end of a wooden handle. This was used with the down-hearth in the position illustrated (Fig. 172). A late eighteenth-century example has a three-pronged fork suspended from a universal joint attached to a wooden shaft (171). With the fork so arranged it was only necessary to give the shaft half a turn to reverse the bread. A similar though simplified arrangement has the fork suspended from one axis only (Fig. 175).

The common form of eighteenth-century toasting fork has the three prongs 'staggered,' which enabled the bread to be held more securely (173 and 174). The large four-pronged fork (176) is from Scotland, and shows strong Continental influence: the tightly-wrapped scrolls and the quantity of detail merely for decoration is not characteristic of English smithcraft.

The seventeenth- and eighteenth-century iron flesh fork or ham fork with two or three prongs evolved from the iron three-barbed flesh hook, a common cooking implement of the Roman occupation. The

IRON FLESH HOOK *Roman type*

eighth-century type is shown in Fig. 109, one of the fourteenth century in Fig. 110, while Chaucer's cook is shown with a similar implement.

CHAUCER'S COOK

The comparatively modern type has a shaped handle sometimes enriched with incised lines and punch marks (Fig. 177). Many of these articles show Flemish influence. This is very obvious in Fig. 178: in addition to its elaborate centre *motif* it has a hook at the back of the handle to hang it from an implement rack or rail, which was a most uncommon feature in this country.

Adjustable hooks from which meat was suspended in front of the roasting fires had the length regulated on the hook-and-eye principle (Fig. 182). A more complicated type has two calliper-like claws fitted with compound levers in place of the ordinary hook. Thus the heavier the joint suspended the greater the grip (183). A more simple early nineteenth-century hook works on this principle (181), and the small hook with four loops (180) was used with the bottle jack in Dutch ovens. For hanging game and birds in larders an implement commonly called a Dutch crown was used (Fig. 184). The hooks are attached to a band of wrought iron from which three stretchers arch upwards and meet together, having a ring at the top for suspension. When in use they were hauled up by a rope, which passed over a pulley in the ceiling, and was made fast to a cleat on the wall. One of these crowns is shown in Tenier's *Kitchen*.

Skewer holders, similar to the modern article but more substantial, have been in use from mediæval times; they were made in stout iron plate, and generally decorated with a shaped stem, or by incised or perforated ornament (Figs. 185 to 188). An unusually ornamental seventeenth-century example from Balcombe in Sussex is now in the Museum at Lewes. The stem is broadened out at the top into a flat disc which is perforated, the ornament taking the form of a cross and two lilies: at the top is an eye-hole for hanging, the skewers being suspended from the two horn-like prongs at the bottom (185).

Pewter plates were warmed in front of the open fire upon wrought-iron stands (Figs. 189, 191). The plates were secured by four or more upright spokes fitted to a revolving carrier.

A later type was made on the lines of a Dutch oven (190). The receptacle for the plates is made of tinned or painted sheet iron, supported by three wrought iron legs and carried by a half-hoop handle. It served as a carrier, as well as a plate warmer, and dates from the late eighteenth or early nineteenth century.

For getting up ruffles, flounces, and frills a special implement was used called a goffering or 'tally' iron (Figs. 192 to 195), the latter name being a corruption of 'Italian iron,' after the country from which they were introduced, probably in the early seventeenth century. They were made in a countless number of designs during the eighteenth century. and in various metals or combinations of metals. The manner in which they were used was to heat the barrel by inserting a red-hot bar of iron, in form similar to a poker. These heaters were used in pairs; thus a reserve heater was always in readiness. The linen, having been starched, was grasped in both hands and pressed over the hot barrel which made a semicircular crimp.

The barrels were made in various sizes, ranging from one-quarter of an inch to an inch and a half. In some examples two or more sizes are mounted on the same base (Fig. 204).

For certain work a hand goffering iron was necessary, but they were not common (202 and 203).

During the end of the eighteenth century tally irons became stereotyped in form (Figs. 198 to 201).

For ironing the plain rounded surface of mob caps a standing iron was used. This has a rounded body supported by a stem. In the more elaborate examples the body opened to receive an iron heater (Fig. 205); but in the more common type a solid egg-shaped body served which was thrust into the fire and when of sufficient heat taken out, wiped, and placed in a cast iron circular base (206). With these were also used small solid goffering irons which were heated in the same way, an example being shown in the same illustration.

Box irons, the forerunner of the modern flat iron (Fig. 196), were made hot like tally irons, having an iron heater which was inserted through a door at the larger end. These irons stood upon three-legged stands, made in both iron and brass in a variety of forms (197).

Before the introduction of cube sugar, refined sugar was made in the form of a loaf, a circular cone some fourteen inches at the base by about three feet in height. The salesman would break off what was required in large irregular lumps: these lumps would be broken up in the kitchen into pieces convenient for table use. For this purpose sugar nippers were employed (Fig. 207). These were made on the principle of pliers, the jaws being almost circular and having a sharp blade at the end of each; they could be manipulated by one hand, as the jaws were forced open by a spring upon unfastening a catch at the end of the handles. To prevent the knuckles coming into violent contact with the table upon which the sugar was being broken up a spike or distance piece was attached to the outside of one handle. In some examples (though this is very exceptional) a guard similar to a sword-hilt was provided. They were made in iron and steel, mostly for kitchen use, although a smaller size was produced in burnished steel for the table. Some of the late eighteenth-century patterns have incised ornament upon the flat surfaces where the jaws hinge.

These implements are illustrated in some trade catalogues of the late eighteenth century in the Print Room at the Victoria and Albert Museum. That they obtained well into the last century is proved by the numbers which can still be found in odd shops all over the country.

A similar and rather more elaborate cutter was mounted on a polished mahogany stand, the nippers being supported at the hinge by a turned brass pillar (209).

Sugar hammers were used but not to the same extent (208).

All these implements survived in sweet shops long after they had become obsolete for household use.

Pastry knives or Jiggers have been in common use from the seventeenth century for cutting dough before baking, the double-notched wheel causing a serrated pattern. Seventeenth-century examples have an open-spoked wheel with stem handles ornamented with chamfering or flattened out into a curved blade (Fig. 210). Those of the eighteenth century have solid wheels with a shaped cutter at the end of the handle for making ornamental devices (211 and 212). They were usually made of cast brass, but wrought iron was also used; one in this metal is in the British Museum dating from the early eighteenth century, with spoon handle. Similar implements had tweezers in place of the wheel (213).

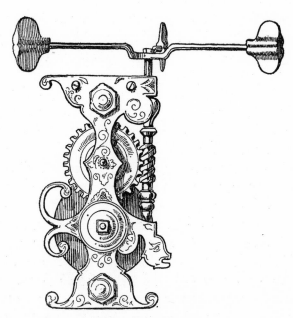

CAST AND ENGRAVED BRASS-FACED SPIT
DRIVING GEAR *17th century*

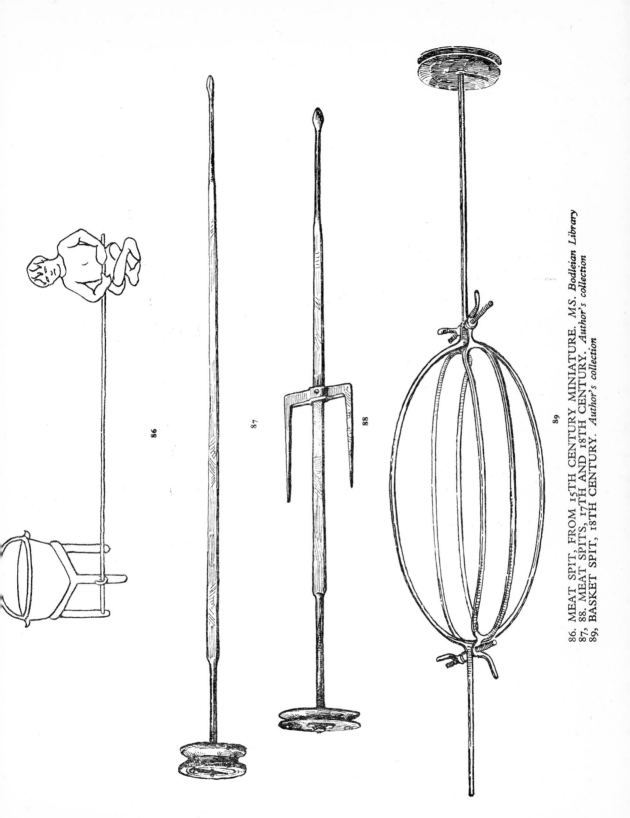

86. MEAT SPIT, FROM 15TH CENTURY MINIATURE. *MS. Bodleian Library*
87, 88. MEAT SPITS, 17TH AND 18TH CENTURY. *Author's collection*
89, BASKET SPIT, 18TH CENTURY. *Author's collection*

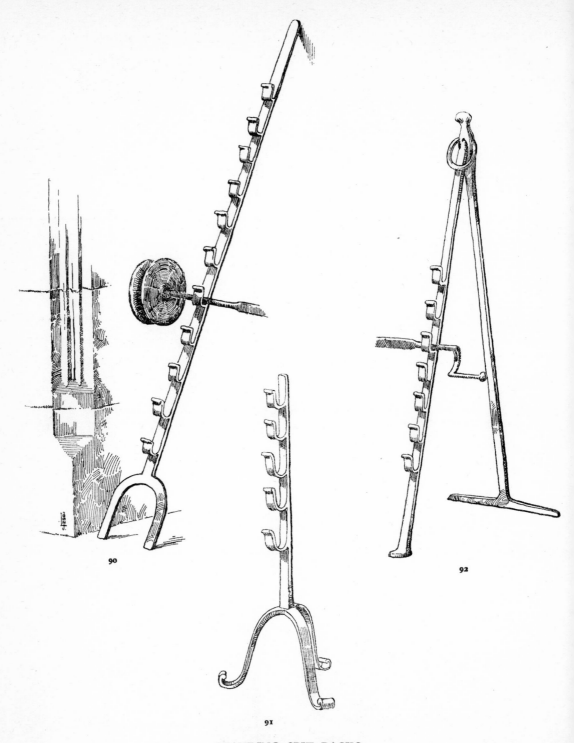

STANDING SPIT RACKS

90. 17TH CENTURY. *From Cotehele House, Cornwall*
91, 92. 18TH CENTURY

**93. DOG DRIVEN SPIT**
*After a drawing by Rowlandson, 1798*

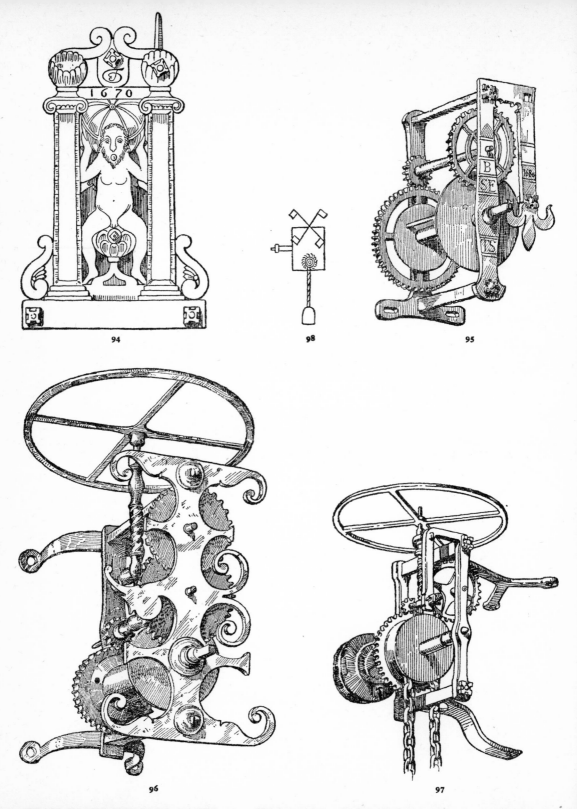

94. BRASS-FACED SPIT JACK, DATED 1670. Height 16½ ins. *Croft-Lyons bequest, Victoria & Albert Museum*
95. WROUGHT-IRON SPIT JACK, DATED 1680. Height 12 ins. *Brighton Museum*
96. WROUGHT-IRON SPIT JACK, 18TH CENTURY TYPE. Height 18 ins. *Author's collection*
97. WROUGHT-IRON SPIT JACK, 18TH CENTURY. Height 13½ ins. *Author's collection*
98. SKETCH OF SPIT JACK. *From the Journal of Timothy Burrell, 1692*

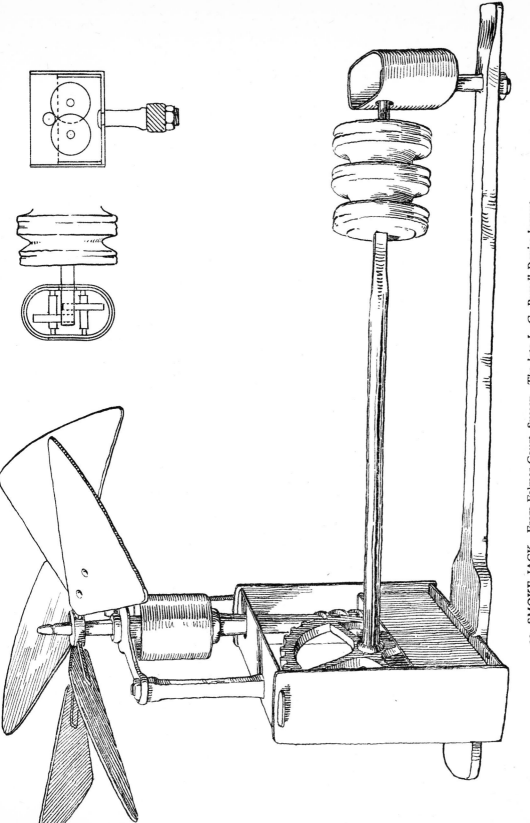

99. SMOKE JACK. From Falmer Court, Sussex. *The late L. G. Russell-Davies bequest*

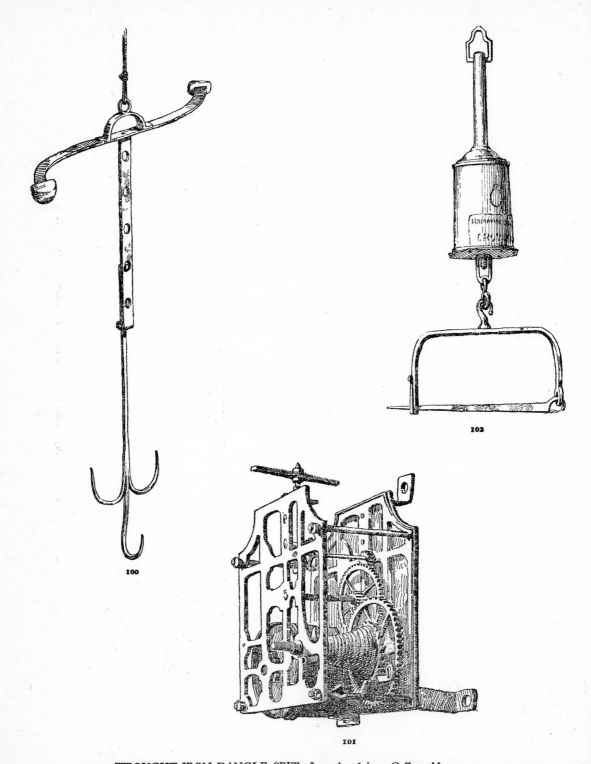

100. WROUGHT-IRON DANGLE SPIT. Length 26 ins. *Geffrye Museum*
101. CLOCK-WORK SPIT JACK. Length 14 ins. *Author's collection*
102. BOTTLE JACK WITH BROCHE SPIT. 21 ins. over all. *Author's collection*

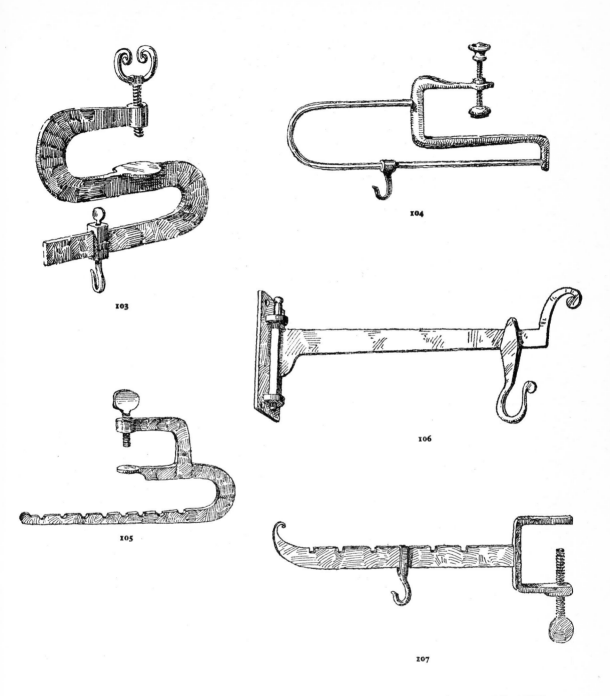

103–107. JACK RACKS, FOR SUSPENDING BOTTLE JACKS AND DANGLE SPITS

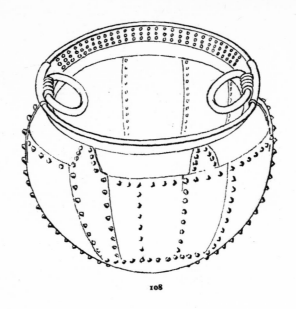

108

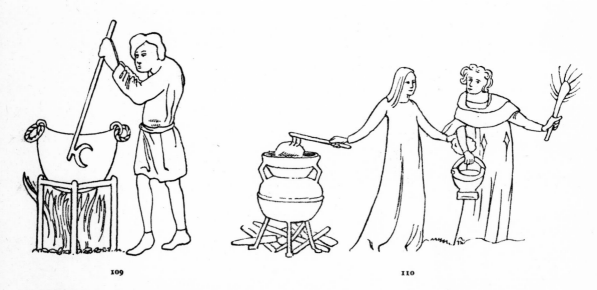

109                                              110

108. BRONZE AGE CAULDRON, 900–100 B.C.
109. CAULDRON AND BRANDRETH OF THE 8TH CENTURY. *Cotton Library, British Museum, B. IV*
110. CAULDRON, 14TH CENTURY. *From MS. Reg. 10 E. IV*

111. BRONZE CAULDRON, 14TH–15TH CENTURY TYPE
Height 15 ins. *National Museum of Antiquities, Edinburgh*

112. BRONZE CAULDRON, 14TH–15TH CENTURY TYPE
*British Museum*

113   114

115   116

113-115. CAST-IRON CAULDRONS, 15TH CENTURY TYPE. *National Museum of Antiquities, Edinburgh*
116. BRONZE VESSEL FOR HOLDING WATER, 15TH CENTURY TYPE. *British Museum*

117

118

119

120

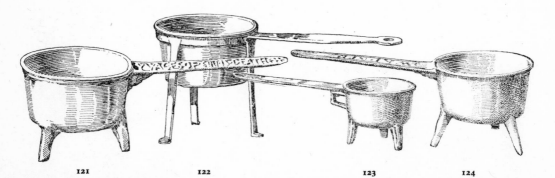

121 122 123 124

117–119. SKILLET HANDLES
120. SKILLETS OR POSNETS, 15TH CENTURY TYPE. Heights 6 ins. and 4½ ins. *Guildhall Museum*
121. BELL-METAL SKILLET. Length 16½ ins. *British Museum*
122. BRASS SKILLET IN WROUGHT-IRON STAND. Length 16 ins. *Author's collection*
123, 124. BELL-METAL SKILLETS. *Author's collection*

125. BRASS JUG, 15TH CENTURY TYPE. Height 10 ins. *National Museum of Antiquities, Edinburgh*
126. BRONZE EWER, 14TH CENTURY TYPE. *British Museum*
127. BRONZE EWER, 14TH–15TH CENTURY TYPE. *British Museum*
128. BRONZE EWER, 14TH CENTURY. Height 21 ins. *British Museum*

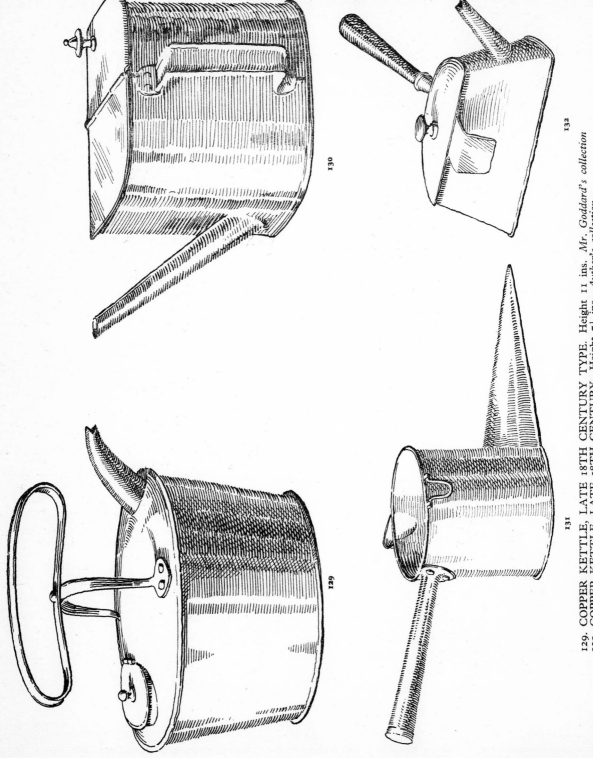

129. COPPER KETTLE, LATE 18TH CENTURY TYPE. Height 11 ins. *Mr. Goddard's collection*
130. COPPER KETTLE, LATE 18TH CENTURY. Height 7¼ ins. *Author's collection*
131, 132. COPPER ALE WARMERS, LATE 18TH-19TH CENTURY TYPE. *Mr. C. M. Escaré's collection*

133. BRONZE MORTAR. Height 8½ ins. *Victoria & Albert Museum*
134. CAST-IRON MORTAR, LATE 17TH CENTURY. Height 6½ ins. *Brighton Museum*
135. CAST-IRON MORTAR, EARLY 18TH CENTURY. Height 6 ins. *Brighton Museum*
136. CAST-IRON MORTAR, LATE 18TH CENTURY. Height 5 ins. *Mr. C. M. Escaré*
137. CAST-BRONZE PESTLE, 17TH CENTURY. Length 10 ins. *Author's collection*

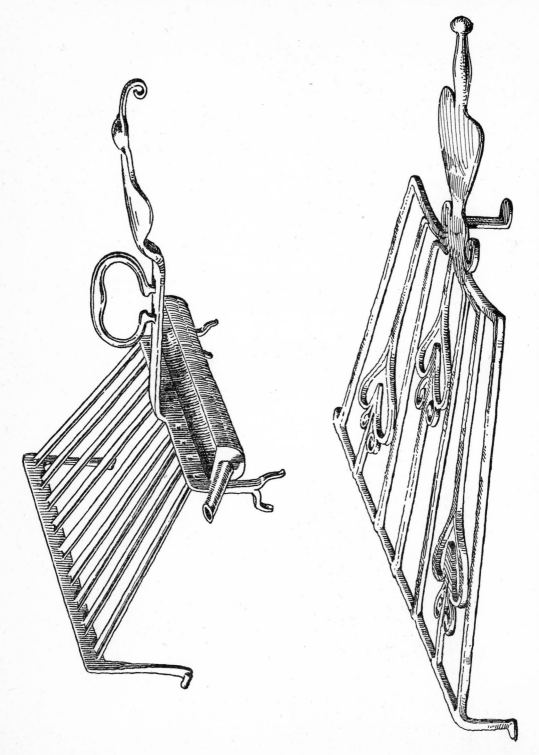

138. GRIDIRON, LATE 18TH CENTURY. Length 18 ins.  Mr. C. M. Escaré's collection
139. GRIDIRON, 17TH–18TH CENTURY TYPE. Length 21¾ ins.  Victoria & Albert Museum

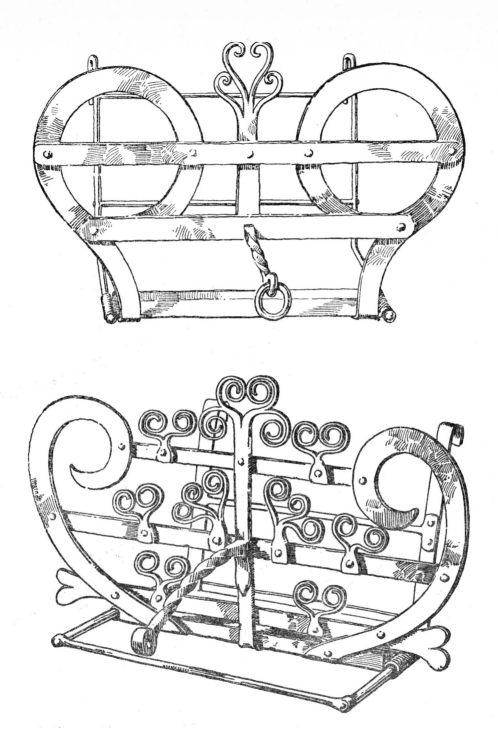

140. SCOTTISH TOASTER, 17TH CENTURY. Width 22½ ins. *Victoria & Albert Museum*
141. SCOTTISH TOASTER, 17TH CENTURY. Width 24 ins. *From Edinburgh*

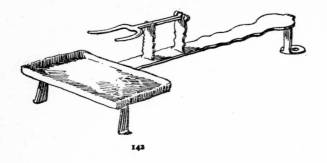

142

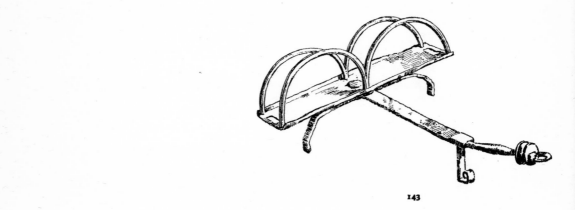

143

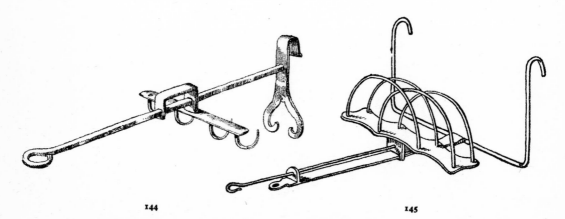

144

145

142. DOWN-HEARTH TOASTER, 17TH–18TH CENTURY TYPE. *Victoria & Albert Museum*
143. DOWN-HEARTH TOASTER, 17TH–18TH CENTURY TYPE. *Geffrye Museum*
144. FIRE-BAR TOASTER, 18TH CENTURY. *The late L. G. Russell-Davies bequest*
145. FIRE-BAR TOASTER, LATE 18TH CENTURY. *The late L. G. Russell-Davies bequest*

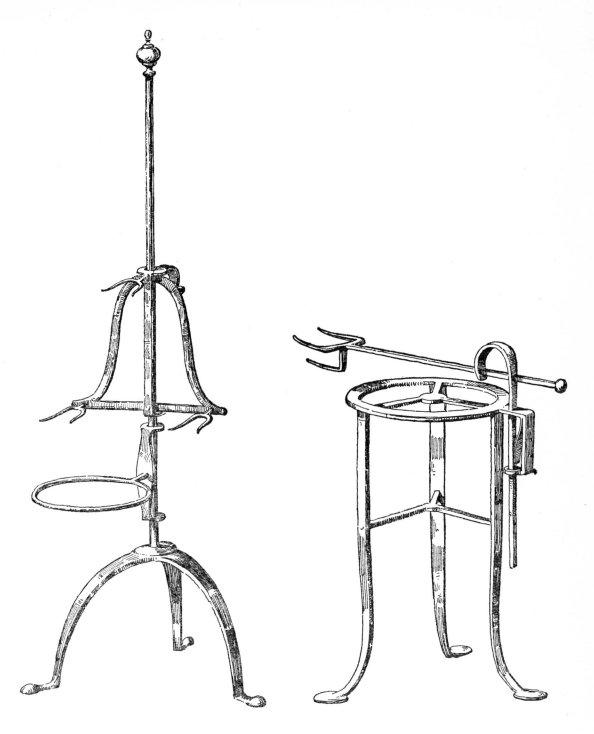

146. STANDING TOASTER, 18TH CENTURY. Height 29 ins. *Messrs. J. F. Garrod, Ltd.*
147. TRIVET TOASTER, 18TH CENTURY. Height 15 ins. *Victoria & Albert Museum*

148. WAFERING IRONS, 16TH CENTURY. *The late L. G. Russell-Davies bequest*
149. WAFERING IRONS, 17TH–18TH CENTURY TYPE. Length 2 ft. 1½ ins.

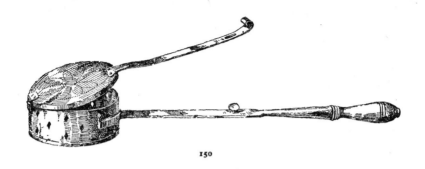

150. CHESTNUT ROASTER, 18TH CENTURY. Length 30 ins. *The late L. G. Russell-Davies bequest*
151. COFFEE ROASTER, 18TH–19TH CENTURY TYPE. Length 31½ ins. *Author's collection*
152. WARMING-PAN, 17TH CENTURY. Length 36 ins. *Victoria & Albert Museum*
153. COPPER WARMING-PAN WITH WOOD TURNED HANDLE. Length 55 ins. *Author's collection*

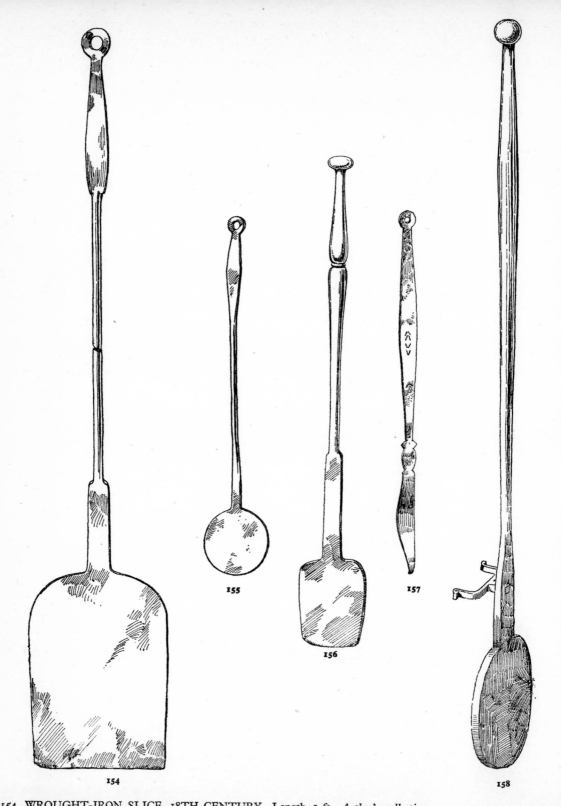

154. WROUGHT-IRON SLICE, 18TH CENTURY. Length 5 ft. *Author's collection*
155. SALAMANDER, 18TH CENTURY. Length 21 ins. *Mr. C. M. Escaré's collection*
156. SALAMANDER, 18TH CENTURY. Length 28½ ins. *The late L. G. Russell-Davies bequest*
157. POTATO RAKE, 18TH CENTURY. Length 21 ins. *Horniman Museum*
158. DOWN-HEARTH SALAMANDER, 17TH CENTURY. Length 3 ft. 7½ ins. *The late L. G. Russell-Davies bequest*

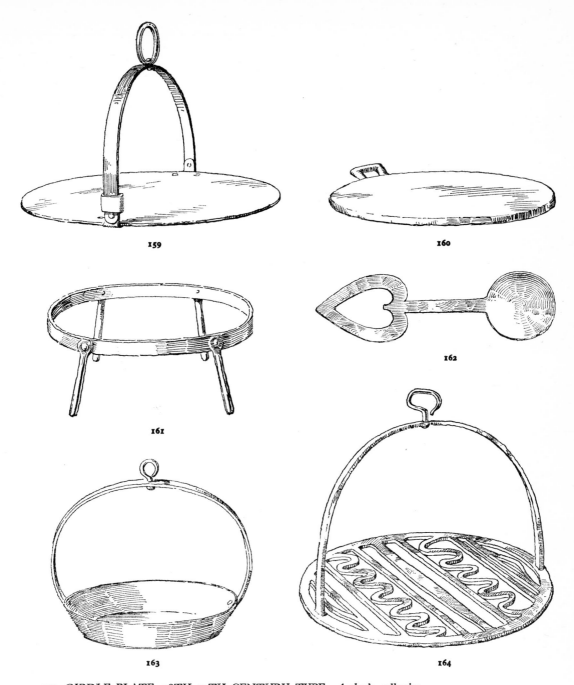

159. GIRDLE PLATE, 18TH–19TH CENTURY TYPE. *Author's collection*
160. GIRDLE PLATE, 17TH CENTURY TYPE. *The late L. G. Russell-Davies bequest*
161. BRANDRETH, 18TH CENTURY TYPE. *The late L. G. Russell-Davies bequest*
162. COMBINED BREAD SPADE AND BASTER. *National Museum of Antiquities, Edinburgh*
163. HANGING FRYING-PAN, 18TH CENTURY TYPE. *The late L. G. Russell-Davies bequest*
164. BRANDER, 18TH CENTURY TYPE. *National Museum of Antiquities, Edinburgh*

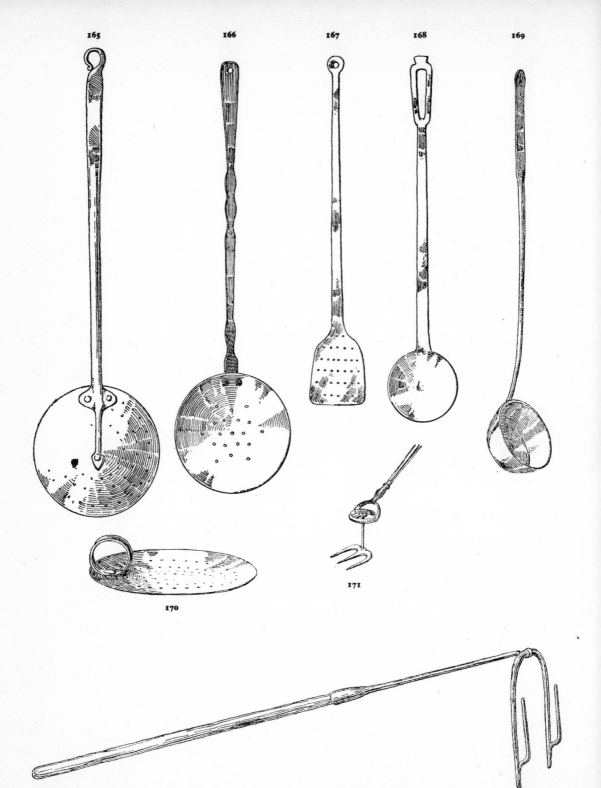

165, 166. SKIMMERS. Lengths 24 ins. and 22½ ins.
167. FISH SLICE. Length 18 ins.
168, 169. LADLES. Lengths 18½ ins. and 20 ins.

170. CREAM SKIMMER
171. SWIVEL TOASTING FORK
172. DOWN-HEARTH BREAD TOASTER.
Length 27 ins.

*All from the Author's collection*

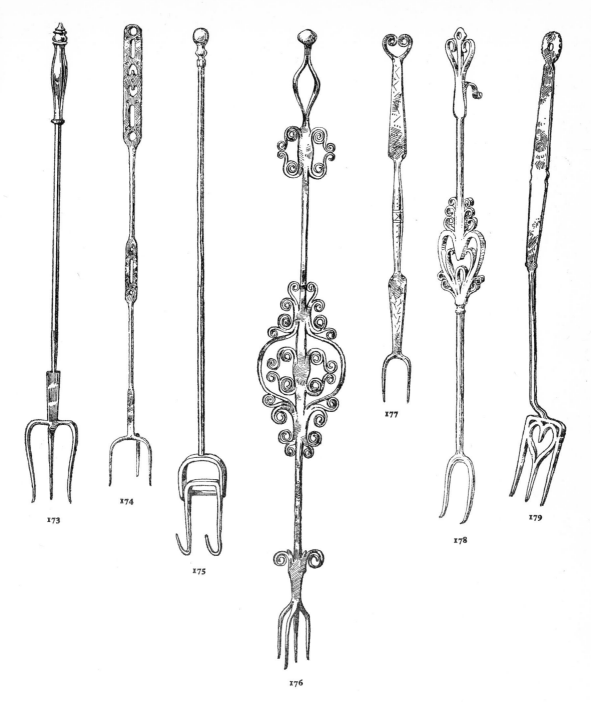

173–175. TOASTING FORKS, 17TH–18TH CENTURY TYPES. *The late L. G. Russell-Davies bequest*
176. TOASTING FORK, 17TH CENTURY TYPE. Length 28 ins. *Royal Scottish Museum, Edinburgh*
177, 178. MEAT FORKS, 17TH CENTURY TYPE. *Mr. Edmondson's collection*
179. MEAT FORK, 17TH CENTURY TYPE. *The late L. G. Russell-Davies bequest*

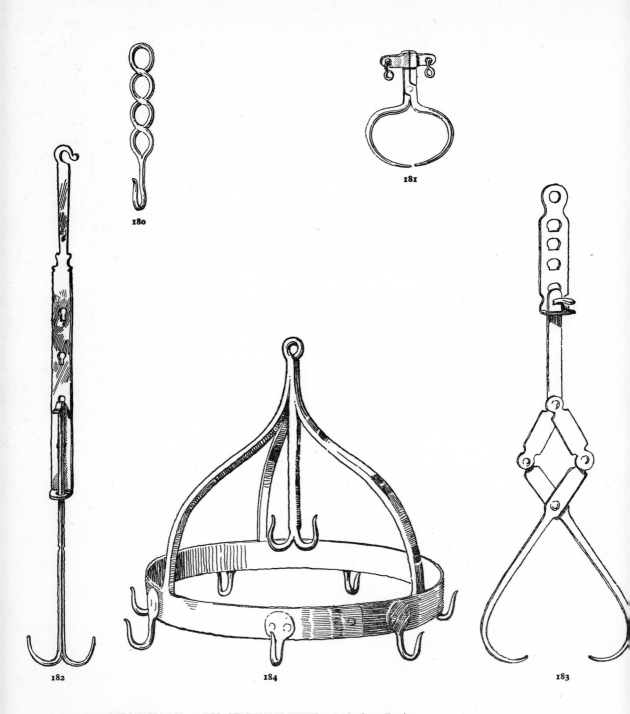

180. MEAT HOOK, 19TH CENTURY TYPE. *Author's collection*
181. MEAT HOOK, 18TH CENTURY TYPE. *The late L. G. Russell-Davies bequest*
182. ADJUSTABLE MEAT HOOK. *Mr. C. M. Escaré's collection*
183. ADJUSTABLE MEAT HOOK. *Victoria & Albert Museum*
184. GAME HANGER (DUTCH CROWN). Width 15 ins. *The late L. G. Russell-Davies bequest*

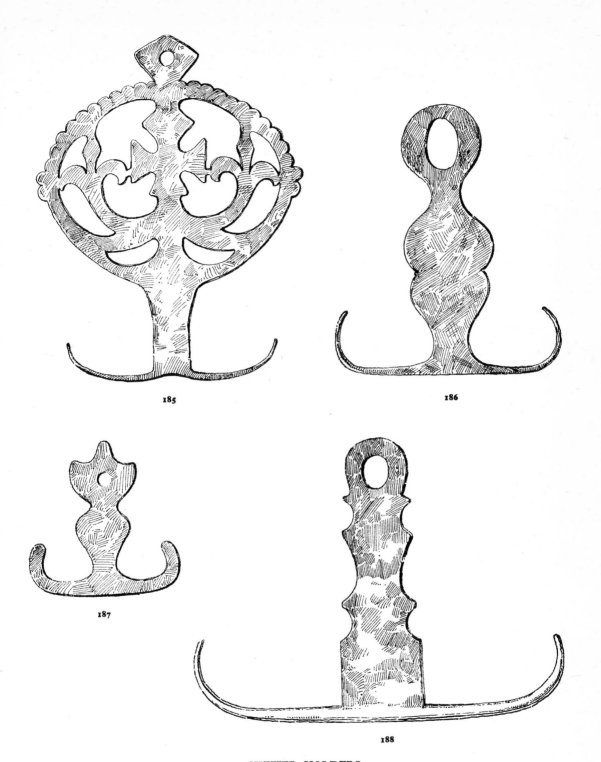

**SKEWER HOLDERS**

185. 17TH CENTURY TYPE. *Lewes Museum*
186. 18TH CENTURY TYPE. *Author's collection*
187, 188. 18TH CENTURY TYPES. *The late L. G. Russell-Davies bequest*

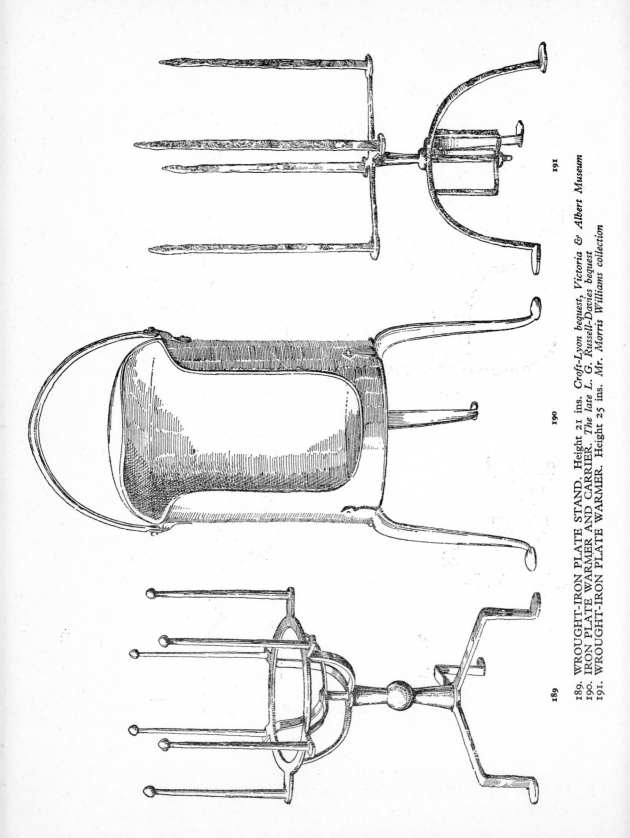

189, WROUGHT-IRON PLATE STAND. Height 21 ins. *Croft-Lyon bequest, Victoria & Albert Museum*
190. IRON PLATE WARMER AND CARRIER. *The late L. G. Russell-Davies bequest*
191. WROUGHT-IRON PLATE WARMER. Height 25 ins. *Mr. Morris Williams collection*

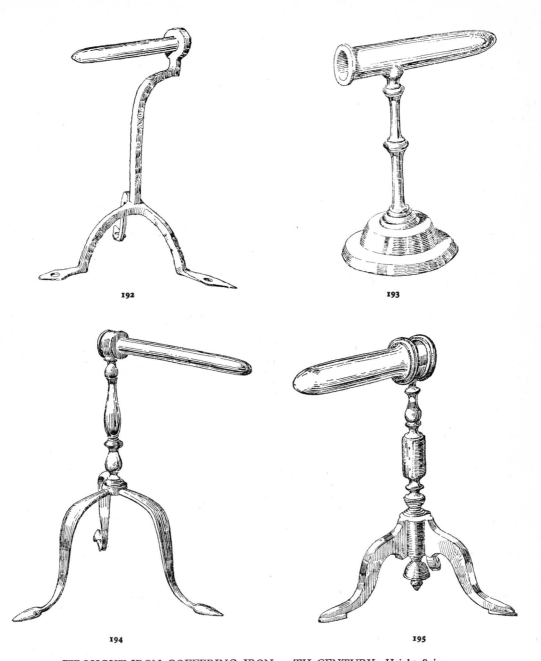

192. WROUGHT-IRON GOFFERING IRON, 17TH CENTURY. Height 8 ins.
193. BRASS GOFFERING IRON, 18TH CENTURY. Height 7 ins.
194. STEEL GOFFERING IRON, EARLY 18TH CENTURY. Height 8¾ ins.
195. IRON GOFFERING IRON ON BRASS STAND, 18TH CENTURY. Height 9½ ins.
*All from Author's collection*

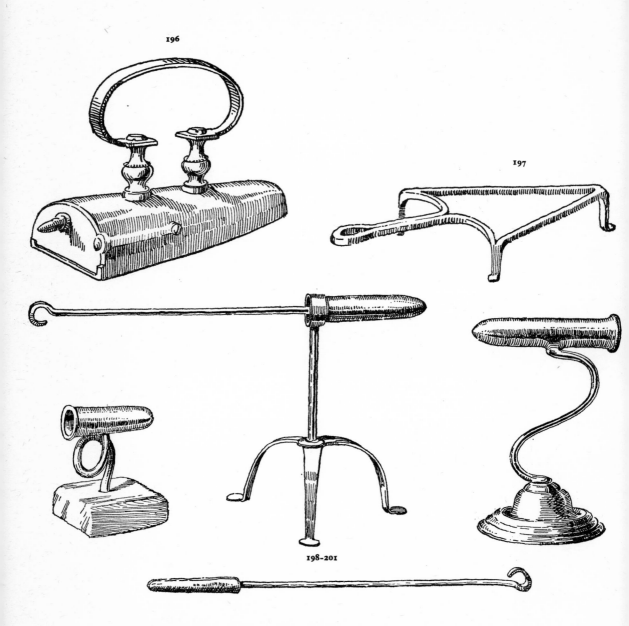

196. BOX IRON AND STAND, 18TH CENTURY. *The late L. G. Russell-Davies bequest*
197. IRON STAND, 19TH CENTURY *Author's collection*
198–201. GOFFERING IRONS, 19TH CENTURY. *Author's collection*

202–3

204

205

206

202, 203. HAND GOFFERING IRON WITH HEATER, EARLY 19TH CENTURY. *Mr. C. M Escaré*
204. DOUBLE GOFFERING IRON ON BRASS PILLARS ON CAST-IRON BASE, EARLY 19TH CENTURY
Height 10½ ins. *Mr. C. M. Escaré*
205. STANDING IRON WITH BRASS TOP, EARLY 19TH CENTURY. Height 14 ins. *Mr. C. M. Escaré*
206. STANDING IRON, CAST IRON, MID 19TH CENTURY. *Author's collection*

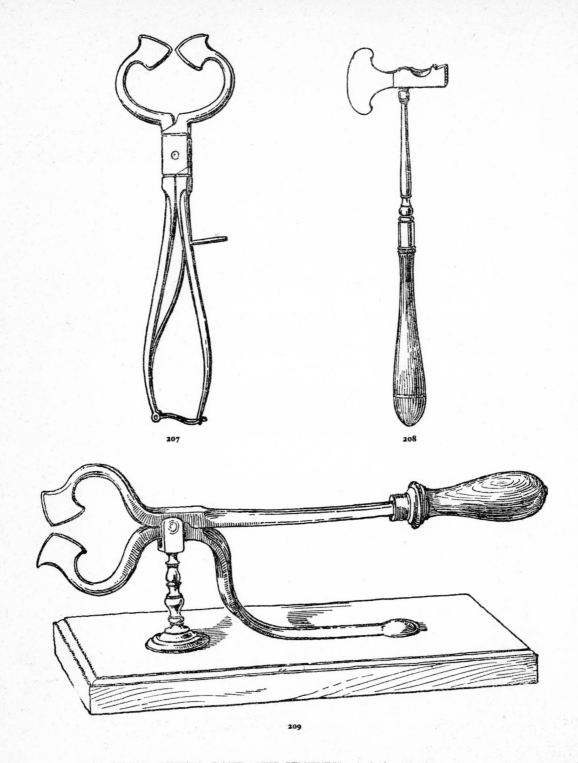

207. SUGAR NIPPERS, LATE 18TH CENTURY. *Author's collection*
208. SUGAR HAMMER, LATE 18TH CENTURY. *Mr. C. M. Escaré's collection*
209. SUGAR CUTTER ON WOOD STAND, 18TH CENTURY. *Author's collection*

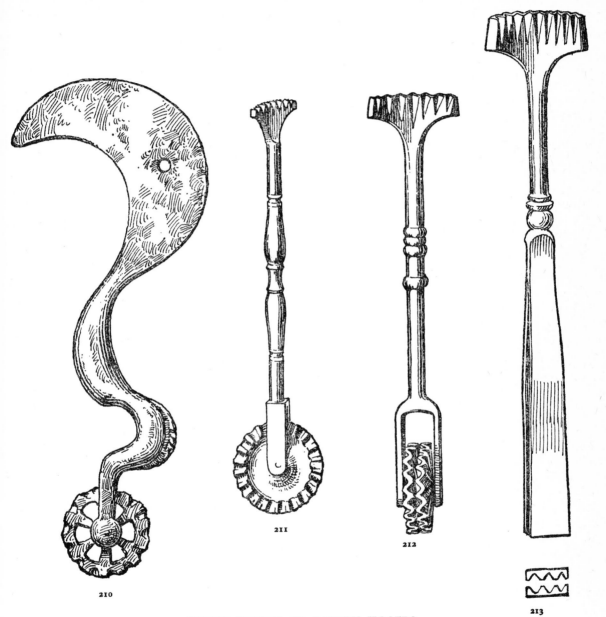

**COOKS' KNIVES OR PASTRY JIGGERS**

210. 17TH CENTURY TYPE. *British Museum*
211, 213. 18TH CENTURY TYPES. *Author's collection*
212. 18TH CENTURY TYPE. *Mr. H. Leonard Ashford*

# PART THREE

# ARTIFICIAL LIGHT

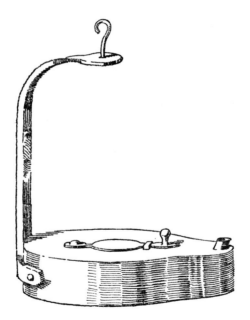

IRON PENDANT LAMP FOR FISH OR COLSER OIL
*eighteenth—nineteenth century*

# ARTIFICIAL LIGHT

ARTIFICIAL LIGHT FOR domestic use was obtained from three sources—solid fat coated upon a wick, oil burned in lamps, and the wood of the fir tree, long buried in a morass or moss-fallen, split and used as candles. All these methods have obtained from the earliest historical times, but candles must be looked upon as the national illuminant until paraffin was introduced about the middle of the nineteenth century. The method of making candles varied according to the ingredients. The early candles were made of wax or tallow, or a combination of both. It was not till the middle of the eighteenth century that spermaceti was introduced. This was a hard white wax prepared from the blubber of the sperm-whale, and gave a clear even light. One hundred years later came the paraffin wax candle which superseded all other forms for ordinary domestic use.

Wax candles were made by basting the melted wax down a wick of rush, cotton or flax, repeating the operation until it became of a sufficient thickness. They were then rolled whilst still warm upon a wet board or stone slab to give them a smooth surface. It was impossible to cast wax candles in moulds, owing to the great shrinkage of wax on cooling. With tallow candles the wicks were dipped in melted tallow until sufficient fat had adhered to the wick, or cast in moulds of wood or sheet iron. Considerable skill was needed in casting, as the candles would not leave the mould if the fat was too hot.

The moulds (Figs. 217 and 218) are tapered, the wick was stretched down the centre of the tube, fixed at the small end by a plug and at the top to a cross wire. The tallow having been run in and set, the peg was removed and the candle drawn out by its wick. Rushlights were a form of candle but with only a very slight coating of tallow upon the wick.

No better explanation could be given of the rushlight than that which is to be found in Gilbert White's *Natural History of Selborne*. It occurs in a letter dated from Selborne Nov. 1st, 1775.

'His . . . tae dae pingues, hic plurimus ignis
Semper, et assidua postes fuligine nigri.'

'DEAR SIR,

I shall make no apology for troubling you with the detail of a very simple piece of domestic economy, being satisfied that you think nothing beneath your attention that tends to utility: the matter alluded to is the use of rushes instead of candles, which I am well aware prevails in many districts besides this; but as I know there are countries also where it does not obtain, and as I have considered the subject with some degree of exactness, I shall proceed in my humble story, and leave you to judge of the expediency.

The proper species of rush for this purpose seems to be the *juncus effusus*, or common soft rush, which is to be found in most moist pastures, by the sides of streams, and under hedges. These rushes are in best condition in the height of summer; but may be gathered, so as to serve the purpose well, quite on to autumn. It would be needless to add that the largest and longest are best. Decayed labourers, women, and children, make it their business to procure and prepare them. As soon as they are cut, they must be flung into water, and kept there, for otherwise they will dry and shrink, and the peel will not rub. At first a person would find it no easy matter to divest a rush of its peel or rind, so as to leave one regular, narrow, even rib from top to bottom that may support the pith; but this, like other feats, soon becomes familiar even to children, and we have seen an old woman, stone blind, performing this business with great dispatch, and seldom failing to strip them with the nicest regularity. When these *junci* are thus far prepared, they must lie out on the grass to be bleached, and take the dew for some nights, and afterwards be dried in the sun.

Some address is required in dipping these rushes in the scalding fat or grease; but this knack also is to be obtained by practice. The careful wife of an industrious Hampshire labourer obtains all her fat for nothing; for she saves the scummings of her bacon-pot for this use; and, if the grease abounds with salt, she causes the salt to precipitate to the bottom, by setting the scummings in a warm oven. Where hogs are not much in use, and especially by the seaside the coarser animal oils will come very cheap. A pound of common grease may be procured for fourpence, and about six pounds of rushes, medicated and ready for use, will cost three shillings. If men that keep bees will mix a little wax with the grease, it will give it a consistency, and render it more cleanly, and make the rushes burn longer; mutton suet would have the same effect.

A good rush, which measured in length two feet four inches and a half, being minuted, burnt only three minutes short of an hour; and a rush of still greater length has been known to burn one hour and a quarter.

These rushes give a good clear light. Watch-lights (coated with tallow), it is true, shed a dismal one, 'darkness visible'; but then the wick of those have two ribs of the rind, or peel, to support the pith, while the wick of the dipped rush has but one. The two ribs are intended to impede the progress of the flame and make the candle last.

In a pound of dry rushes, avoirdupois, which I caused to be weighed and numbered, we found upwards of one thousand six hundred individuals. Now suppose each of these burns, one with another, only half an hour, then a poor man will purchase eight hundred hours of light, a time exceeding thirty-three entire days, for three shillings. According to this account each rush, before dipping, costs $\frac{1}{33}$ of a farthing, and $\frac{1}{11}$ afterwards. Thus a poor family will enjoy five and a half hours of comfortable light for a farthing. An experienced old housekeeper assures me that one pound and a half of rushes completely supplies his family the year round, since working people burn no candles in the long days, because they rise and go to bed by daylight.

Little farmers use rushes much in the short days both morning and evening, in the dairy and kitchen; but the very poor, who are always the worst economists, and therefore must continue very poor, buy a halfpenny candle every evening, which in their blowing open rooms, does not burn much more than two hours. Thus have they only two hours' light for their money instead of eleven. . . .'

In the *Privy Purse Expenses* of Henry the Eighth under the year 1529 there are these two entries:

'Item for a potell of salet oyle . . . . ijs. iiijd.
Item for a botell and for Russhes to brenne w^t the
    saied oyle . . . . . . . iijd.'

So it seems that one method of making rushlights was to soak the rush in oil in place of the coating of tallow.

An eighteenth-century implement for dipping rush wicks is similar in form to the candle mould (219). The usual method for making them was to melt the fat in a boat-shaped utensil of cast iron mounted on three short legs and with a long handle similar to a skillet (214). The rush was then drawn through the fat once or twice and placed on sheets of bark to dry in the open. When the candle tax was imposed in 1709, the home-made candle was forbidden and all implements connected with their making was hidden or destroyed. So that the revenue should not be diminished by the substitution of oil, all oil lamps for domestic use were prohibited (with the exception of lamps burning fish oil) under a penalty of two pounds.

In the great halls of the Middle Ages artificial illumination was provided by candles or torches, the latter being impaled upon iron spikes, or held in openwork cages or cressets. A well wrought example of a cresset and frame of a type used in the great houses of the early Tudor period is shown in Fig. 220. This was carried on a pole handle and could be used in the Great Hall or carried by the watch patrol.

Candles were supported by candle pendants called candle beams (Fig. 221), candle brackets (222), and standards (224). Candle staffs were also held by servants during any ceremony where additional light was required (223). Three of these illustrations occur in a miniature of the fifteenth century (B.M. Reg. 18 E. 11) and the fourth from B.M. M.S. Egerton 2125, dated 1500.

Candle beams were usually of wood with iron or brass pans for the candles.

Few mediæval wrought-iron candle supports have been preserved excepting those which have been excavated from time to time. The City of London is fortunate in having several examples now in the Guildhall Museum.

The early method of supporting the large and medium-sized candles was to thrust them upon a pricket or spike. They were often supplied with a hole in the base for this purpose, and were known as 'pricket candles.' Small candles needed more support, so nozzles were provided in some cases. The wrought-iron pendant for two candles (Fig. 228), the bracket (225) and the standard (226), all fifteenth- and sixteenth-century types, are provided with nozzles, the last having also a pricket. The table spike with two side prongs or clips functioned as both pricket and rush clip (227).

As domestic conditions became more comfortable, artificial lighting became greatly extended and numerous implements were made for this purpose. In the lesser houses of the seventeenth and eighteenth centuries the rush holder, or combined rush and candle holder, was universal. The most common method of holding the rushlight was by a hinged clip mounted upon a stem, one of the jaws being carried on as a candle nozzle (Fig. 229) or with a counterweight (230). For table use the stems were usually supported upon a wooden base but the more ornamental had three metal legs. Another type has the jaws closed by a steel spring. With some of these the jaws were fashioned to hold either rush or candle (231). Chamfering and incised lines were sometimes used in the scheme of decoration (232). Two types of table rush holders are shown in Figs. 233 and 234; in the former a double rush holder with spring clip made of light sheet iron and standing on a turned wood base, and in the latter a two-light candle holder with counterweight rush clip. The stem is connected to the flat ring base by four curved and twisted legs. A most unusual type.

A simple device for holding a rush was a steel spring clip mounted upon a wooden base (Figs. 235 and 237). A crude portable variety has an iron candle socket, at the side of which is a prong for the rush; the lower end of the stem is turned at right angles into a wooden base, part of which is fashioned to form a handle (236).

Floor standards of this period were of wrought iron, or had an iron stem supported by a wooden base. The usual type had a rush clip or

44

combined rush and candle holder fitted to a carrier, which slid up and down the stem, being held in the required position by a friction spring (Figs. 238 and 239). Another kind of standard had a small rush or candle holder fixed upon a wooden stand, the stem being made of two uprights, one fixed to the base, and the other, which supported the holder, constructed to slide up and down on the ratchet principle (240). The two examples shown in Figs, 241 and 242 have adjustable lights. Fig. 241 is on the pot-hook ratchet principle, a most unusual method. Fig. 242 is the usual type with sliding carriage working on a stem which is held in a heavy wood base.

Standards for use in workshops were only made with candle nozzles, as a rush would not give sufficient light. The height of the candle was adjusted in a similar way, with the arms jointed to give a variable extension (Fig. 244). This example was in use in a cobbler's shop in Leicester, the spike at the bottom of the stem being driven into the earth floor. The reading standard for two candles has the sliding carrier controlled by two friction springs, and stood upon four legs (Fig. 243).

The most common type of pendants in this class of lighting implement has the length adjustable on the ratchet principle, similar to, though much lighter, than pot hooks. They were made with rush clips only (Fig. 245) and for both rush and candle (246 and 247). Other forms of adjustable pendants worked with a hook and eye (Fig. 253), or with a friction spring (254 and 255).

The two small 'S' hook candle pendants (251 and 252) were used in the eighteenth and nineteenth centuries in out-buildings, barns and workshops. An example of the former variety is in the Debtor's Cell at the London Museum. In addition to rush clips and candle sockets, some of these implements had a four-pronged pricket attached to the grease pan. This was for holding a stump of candle after it had burned down too low for use in a socket, and for this reason was called a 'save-all' (252).

The example shown in Fig. 248 was used in the fish houses in Great Yarmouth and district. The fish house dating from the seventeenth century was a rectangular building divided by one or more partitions running longways and formed of slats. Upon these slats the split herrings were suspended from tenter hooks and so smoked by the oak sawdust smouldering on the floor, thus being transformed into kippers. The illustration shows a pendant light for a candle with a 'save-all' to accommodate the stub. The side spike was driven into the frame of the louvres.

A form of candle fitting for one light was used in the north Irish linen industry. This was known as a loom light. The one illustrated in Fig. 249 is a simple twisted stem hook-end type, and that in Fig. 250 is of a similar device but with a cross bar to prevent swinging.

The mediæval method of lighting by wall brackets is illustrated in Fig. 222. During the Stuart period the repoussé silver sconce became fairly fashionable in important houses, and candle arms were fixed to the frames of mirrors and small mirror sconces. In the lesser houses and cottages, wall lighting was never a common feature; the only type of rush and candle holder for this purpose is the wall spike, which has the stem bent at right angles and finished in a spike for driving into a wall or beam (Fig. 257). A more elaborate appliance for candles has a double adjustment, as the arm extends in six joints and is attached to a carrier which slides upon a vertical stem, the bottom end being fixed to the wall (256). This form of lighting was used more in the workshop than in the house. The wrought-iron sconce for two candles with elaborate backplate from Edinburgh shows a strong French or Flemish influence in the treatment of the scrolls (258).

Contemporary with this class of rush and candle holder was the Scottish 'peerman,' an implement used for holding candle-fir: it was evolved from a stone with a hole in the centre in which a cleft stick was fixed. In the National Museum of Antiquities, Edinburgh, there are several examples of these wrought-iron holders (Figs. 259 to 261). The floor standard (259) has, in addition to the clip for candle-fir, a nozzle for an ordinary candle and a hook from which a crusie lamp could be suspended. The carrier slides upon the vertical stem. Wall brackets (260) and table standards (261) were made merely to hold candle-fir. The latter has a double clip upon a wooden stem in which is fixed an iron blade; this was for splitting the candle-fir, an operation usually performed by a fir-fettle or large knife.

The secular candlestick of great houses, throughout the Middle Ages, was the brass or bronze pricket, the most notable being the eleventh-century moulded bronze-gilt example known as the 'Gloucester candlestick,' now in the Victoria and Albert Museum. This design is exceptional, and cannot be regarded as a type. The prevailing mediæval pattern is shown in two miniatures in a fourteenth-century MS. Both the table standard (A) and the floor standard (B) are similar to a type of

A & B. CANDLESTICKS, 14TH CENTURY.    *From Miniatures in MS. B.M., Add. 10293*

church candlestick which has obtained down to the present day; this was the parent of the baluster socketed candlestick. Socketed candlesticks date from the fourteenth century and may have been inspired by Persia and other near Eastern countries, where their use was fairly general at this period.

During the Middle Ages, the Flemish founders made a great number of candlesticks which came to this country, this importation having a marked influence on English design. Strangely free, however, is the brass example in the British Museum (Fig. 262). The grease catcher is in the form of a disc half-way down the stem, the base circular with flanged tray and the lower edge of the foot engraved with the inscription:

'In My Beginnyng God Be My——'

More on Flemish lines is the other example of this period (263) with large grease pan in the centre of the stem.

Of the seventeenth century, two types are conspicuous. One was made in a variety of sizes ranging from twelve to four inches in height, and still retained the grease flange at the base of the long nozzle (264). The other was not of large size, and had no grease pan, except that provided in the circular tray base (265).

In the seventeenth century, slides were introduced in the stems of candlesticks for regulating the height of the candle or ejecting the stump. They were of two forms, a friction spring working on the inner surface of the nozzle and manipulated by a thumb piece, and a 'lift' working in a series of bayonet catches; the latter method is shown in a large sheet brass candlestick with circular tray base (Fig. 266) and also

47

in another sheet brass example, which has the long socket stem and grease pan supported by a walnut base (267). Both are carried by a cast brass hook attached to the top of the nozzle. This form was superseded by the cast baluster type (Figs. 268 to 273), made in great quantities throughout the eighteenth century. During the earlier part of that period the spring slide was still used for clearing the stump, the stems being cast in halves and brazed together (268 to 270). Later the slide was replaced by a central rod worked from under the base and the stems cast in one piece (271 to 273).

Late Georgian kitchen candlesticks (Figs. 274 to 277) were made in sheet iron of which 275 and 276 is the most common type. Fig. 274 is less usual, as it has a cast-iron base and no slide. The other example (277) was used in offices for melting sealing-wax: extra stability is obtained by the base being filled with silver sand.

Candlesticks to hold more than one light were not common in England, but a standard somewhat on the lines of those of the French Empire were in use in banks and offices before the introduction of gas (Fig. 278). These had a circular sand-weighted base, and with the exception of the brass stem were made of Japanned iron relieved with gold lines. The two arms moved up and down the stem, controlled by a friction spring. The shades were regulated independently in a similar manner. Another form of multiple brass stick was for three candles (279), the two side arms folding outwards on three joints adding twelve inches to the spread.

Metal bedroom candlesticks were of two forms, the sheet brass tray, square and round on plan with cast side handle, which usually accommodated an extinguisher (Fig. 282), and the perforated cup type with cylindrical glass shade (280 and 281). With this pattern an extinguisher with long handle was used. The frying-pan form, so common on the Continent, was not much used in this country.

Wax taper stands belong to the seventeenth and eighteenth centuries, the more recent having a pair of spring jaws upon a stem, the latter forming the spool upon which the taper was coiled (283). This design is illustrated in the Trade Pattern Books in the print room at the Victoria and Albert Museum. Their place was upon the writing-tables of the late eighteenth century, when they were used to melt wax for sealing letters.

Candle holders for use in stables had the light protected by six vertical rods, held at the top by a ring and supported by a wooden base (Fig. 284). The candle flame is thus partly protected from stray litter and straw. This principle is of German origin. Another common continental pattern is the spiral candle holder (Fig. 286). This is made of a flat strip of iron wound in the form of a hollow spiral, the edges being sufficiently far apart to allow a 'lift' to move up and down, and so regulate the height of the candle. The continental examples upon this principle are almost always made of round or half-round section iron and mounted upon a metal tray supported on three legs.

Another form is that used in wine cellars (285). With this the iron handle was so made that it could be thrust in a crevice in the wall or between the hoops of a barrel, so leaving both hands free for drawing the liquor.

The early form of candelabra was the candle beam already referred to and illustrated in Fig. 221. Contemporary with this form of lighting was the brass or laten type with six or twelve branches, examples of which may be seen in the Victoria and Albert Museum and the Geffrye Museum. These may have been made in this country, but more probably they were imported from the Low Countries, as the type is much more continental than English. There is an interesting example of this kind from St. Katherine's Hospital, Regent's Park, which has a Gothic body but with the flamboyant arms replaced by those of a more restrained design, typically English, of the seventeenth century (Fig. 287). In addition to this change of candle arms, the six top motifs, which consisted of ornamental branches, but with no candle sockets, have been removed and classical busts fitted in their place.

The most common form of candelabra of the seventeenth century was modelled after Dutch patterns, so often seen in pictures of the period. These had a number of branches attached to a baluster stem, which finished in a large sphere. This form underwent a slight change at the beginning of the eighteenth century, when the arms were attached to the sphere instead of springing from a secondary body just above it (Fig. 289). A small engraving in Randle Holme's *Academy of Armory* (1688) shows the arms treated in this manner (288). Gadrooning was also introduced in the decoration of the bodies. An iron six-branch pendant of primitive design has the nozzles and arms made in one piece and decorated by cable twist, all the arms springing from a common weld and suspended from a small eye (Fig. 290). A similar type had plain iron scroll arms of a small round section grouped round a turned wood body to which they were attached by iron staples.

The example shown (291) originally had six arms and of the remaining three the candle nozzles and pans are missing. The body was painted dark green, with the exception of the carved flame which was leaf gilt.

Oil lamps fashioned after the Roman type have been used in Great Britain from Saxon times and continued throughout the Middle Ages down to the nineteenth century. The most common form is the pendant double-valve lamp used throughout Europe, but each country showed a slight variation in design.

In Scotland, where they continued in use longer than elsewhere, they are known as 'crusie' lamps (Fig. 292), in the Shetlands as 'collies,' in Cornwall as 'chills' (293), and in the Channel Islands as 'cressets' (294). The top valve or container held the oil, and was suspended from a notched rack; this enabled it to be tilted forward as the oil diminished. The lower container held the oil that syphoned over the top lip. Most of these lamps were made of iron, the valves being hammered out and shaped upon dies. The Cornish example (293) is of sheet copper and constructed to burn four wicks.

Crusies to burn more than one wick are shown in Figs. 295 to 297. A 'four wick' (295) has copper valves with iron frame. The suspension hook was so made that they could be either hung from the ceiling, or from the wall by driving in the spike. Stands were also provided, which enabled them to be used as table lamps (298). A combined lamp and candlestick for cellar or outhouse use had the nozzle fixed in the centre of the valve, the handle fashioned as a spike which could be inserted in a crack or crevice (297).

Copper lamps were made in England on similar lines to the crusie, but with only one valve; the wick rested in a shallow trough fixed inside the container, and free from the edge, which prevented the oil draining over the side. The example shown is tinned to prevent corrosion (Fig. 299).

The material used in these crude lamps was usually fish oil obtained from the livers of cod, hake, ling or herring. The wicks were of pith, moss, hemp or cotton. They burnt with an offensive smell, and their use is generally associated with the humbler dwellings.

Oil lamps did not make the headway in this country that they did on the Continent, where much attention was paid to their improvement. This was probably owing to the candle tax of 1709, already referred to, which prohibited all oil lamps, with the exception of those burning fish oil, and which was not repealed until 1831. For common use the only improvement was the spout lamp with closed container. These are made of thin sheet iron or brass (Figs. 300 to 303). The pendant (300) has a curved handle pierced with a number of holes: the suspension hook by engaging in these in succession throws the lamp forward as the oil diminishes. Other forms are the wall lamp (301) and the standard (303) with sand-weighted base similar to, though less elaborate, than the contemporary Dutch examples.

HAND LANTERN, DATE 1500
*From MS. Egerton 2125, British Museum*

The lantern may be described as a screen with transparent panels of horn, skin or glass, used for protecting an illuminating flame from wind or rain. The name is derived from the Latin *lanterna*, the name lanthorn being a sixteenth-century corruption. There are three kinds— hanging, wall, and hand lanterns; of these the hand type was by far the most common, being in constant use from the Conquest. In the Ashmolean Museum, Oxford, there is a fine specimen of this period, the lighting areas being composed of gems. The circular type with dome top survived for many centuries, and one dating from the late fifteenth century occurs in a miniature in the British Museum, here illustrated. Mediæval lanterns are very rare, but two existing examples in sheet bronze of the fourteenth-fifteenth century are shown in Figs. 304 and 305. Both designs are unmistakably of their period, and were for hand use.

Reference to lanterns are fairly general in early Household Expenses; the two following are from the Privy Purse Accounts of the Lestranges of Hunstanton.

'1525
Item pd. to Robt. Rede for iiij lantens                    xij.

1533
Item pd. for a lantarn to hang at the dresser             vj'

A form of small hand lantern for candles which dates from the end of the seventeenth century was of sheet brass decorated with repoussé ornament in Flemish taste (Figs. 306 and 307). Both the examples shown are glazed with roundels set in brass rims, which conform to the irregularity of the glass. These roundels or 'Bull's-Eyes' were a product of the glass industry. Early window glass was made by taking a blob of the molten metal on a rod and rotating rapidly, the centrifugal force causing the glass to be thrown outward in the form of a disc. The rod was removed and the flat portion cut off and used for glazing purposes, the centre hub or roundel being only fit for unimportant windows or lanterns. The larger example is from Whitley; this has, in addition to the usual ventilating perforation in the roof, a short chimney; the other, from Edinburgh, is less elaborate but the treatment of decoration is very similar. An early nineteenth-century travelling lantern with horn panel has a telescopic cowel and wire handles that fold back upon the body (308). A survival of this kind of small hand lamp is that which was used by mid-nineteenth century lamplighters (309). This has a glass panelled door, and held a small oil lamp, the ventilating crown being raised and perforated.

To travel at night upon foot before the introduction of street lighting was, at all periods, almost impossible without a lantern. For this purpose many types were made, and as communities grew up and people were abroad more at night the lantern became an indispensable adjunct of every household. An eighteenth-century pattern which was used in this country and other parts of Europe has a circular sheet iron body with conical roof, the light finding its way through slots so worked as to form a pattern, and two or more roundels (Fig. 310). In this example, which was for rough farmhouse use, a candle holder is attached to the roof: this enabled the candle to be shifted to give greater light when used in sheltered places. A Scottish brass lantern with eight horn panels (311) is of barrel form, ornamented by engraved nautical subjects and punch marks; the bands and stays are strengthened by flanges and over the base of the conical roof is engraved 'P. Fairbairn Cove 1750.' Tradition relates that this lantern was used to warn vessels off the rocks at Cove Cockburnspath.

The universal farmhouse type, and one that survives to the present day, has a circular sheet iron body with four horn panels which are protected by wires (Fig. 312). The roof is ventilated by three dormers. They are still made because for stable and cowhouse use it is essential to have a lantern that will stand hard usage and which entirely eliminates the danger of broken glass.

An early nineteenth-century hand lantern, with a lighting area much above the average, has six glass panels held by a light sheet iron frame (313). Two examples of the same period are for burning oil, the smaller (314) has a thick glass cylinder, the lamp being held by a bayonet catch. In the other the light comes through perforated slots (315). When working farm wagons after dark, a variety of large lantern twenty-four inches high was used (Fig. 316). The lighting panels which were of horn occupied two-thirds of the diameter, and three candles were burned at a time. They were fastened to the wagon by straps passed round the top and bottom bands under metal bridges, which kept them in position. Spare candles were carried in a candle-box, attached to the side of the lantern.

A small early Victorian hexagonal hand lantern has three bevelled glass panels and the light increased by a silver-plated reflector (Fig. 317). Folding lanterns of this period were fairly common: they were usually fitted in a sheet iron pocket case, which also carried the candle in a separate compartment (319).

Neither hanging nor wall metal lanterns were often used until the late eighteenth century, when the former were usually made of a six- or eight-sided metal frame glazed with plate glass, and were employed to light halls, passages and stairs of important houses. Metal wall lanterns were usually fixed at entrance gates, lodges, and stables, and consisted of a weather-proof body with two or more glass panels enclosing a candle or small oil lamp (318). The illustration shows a triangular type now in the Victoria and Albert Museum, and said to have been used in connection with the festivities celebrating the victory of Waterloo.

A hand variety in common use in early-Victorian kitchens was the gauze lantern. This had a circular body with the lighting area composed of thin wire gauze (320). A similar, though less common form, has the metal body perforated (322). They were employed in sculleries and outhouses, but were of no use in a high wind. Another implement of this class was the 'hundred eyes,' so called from the round holes with which the drum was perforated. This was placed in bedrooms as a guard for a candle when burnt as a nightlight (321).

The art of creating a burning temperature quickly is quite a modern one, and started with phosphorous-tipped matches, which came into general use about 1833. Nearly half a century before this, however, 'lights' of a kind were being sold, judging by the following advertisement which appeared in the MORNING POST, March 13th, 1788:

> 'For Travellers, Mariners, etc., Promethean Fire and Phosphorus.
> G. Watts respectfully acquaints the Public that he has prepared a large variety of machines of a portable and durable kind with Promethean fire, paper and match enclosed, most admirably calculated to prevent those disagreeable sensations which frequently arise in the dreary hour of midnight from the sudden alarm of thieves, fire or sickness as by procuring an instantaneous light the worst calamities and depredations might often be prevented in families. Experience has likewise proved this invention to be of the first utility to the traveller, mariners, and those people who frequently rise in the night-time as they can with one of these matches procure light instantly without the great expense and danger of burning a lamp or candle.'

These matches were not used to any extent, and the flint and steel, which, during the Iron Age, was the only convenient method for obtaining a light, continued to be used till the introduction of the phosphorous match, when they were gradually superseded.

In a list of apparel, accoutrements, etc., needed by the Earl of Northumberland and his retinue when preparing to join the English army in France in 1513, there occurs this entry:

> 'Item to remember to have fyre yrens, flynte stones, Tinder, and Brimstone in tyme of nede.'

Receptacles for holding tinder-lighting equipment were made in a great number of forms. They were for household use, also to be carried upon the person. The majority were of the former class, and the most usual type is a round brass or tinned iron box with loose lid, with candle nozzle in the centre and a handle at the side, which enabled it to be used as a portable candlestick (Figs. 323 and 324). Similar boxes were sometimes fitted within large bedroom candlesticks (325), the socket being taller with a slide adjustment. An example is in the Bryant and May Museum of fire-making appliances, probably the most comprehensive collection of its kind in the world. They contained the flint, steel, tinder and sulphur matches, all essentials in producing a light. They also had a flat metal disc with loop handle called the 'damper,' to extinguish the tinder when the match had been ignited. The method of using was to hold the steel, which was in the form of a hook or loop, in the left hand a few inches above the tinder and strike it a sharp downward blow with the flint. This action caused a small particle of steel to be knocked off, the friction making it incandescent; this falling upon the tinder ignited it and caused it to smoulder. The sulphur match was then brought in contact with the smouldering tinder which produced the flame. This operation might be performed in ten seconds, or it might take as many minutes, according to the skill of the operator in making and directing the sparks, and also to the age of the tinder, which became almost useless after three or four days.

Breton in 1626 describes the use of the tinder box in the following passage:

> 'The maid is stirring betimes, and slipping on her shooes and her petticoat, groaps for the tinder box, where after a conflict between the steel and the stone, she begets a spark, at last the candle lights on his match; then upon an old rotten foundation of broken boards she erects an artificiall fabrick of the Black Bowels of New-Castle soyle, to which she sets fire with as much confidence as the Romans to their Funeral Pyles.'

Steels were made in great variety, some ornamented types being finely wrought (Figs. 326 to 328). Small tongs were used by smokers to pick up smouldering tinder and place in the pipe bowl, and were sometimes attached to the steel (326).

Pocket tinder boxes were in rectangular form, the sides forming the steel, the lid being opened by releasing a spring catch (329). Tinder was usually made by scorching cotton or linen fabric, although fungus, touchwood, and other vegetable substances have been used.

Sulphur matches were slips of wood with both ends sharpened and dipped in sulphur (331). They went by the name of 'spunks;' this name occurs in G. Wilson's collection of songs:

> 'The Spunks dipt with brimstone he gropt for
> In order to light him a candle
> He imagined his fish was the fire
> But yet not a spark could he kindle.'

In making these matches the sulphur was melted in a tinned iron receptacle, somewhat on the lines of a safety ink-well, it being so formed to keep the melted sulphur from igniting (330).

One form of mechanical tinder box had a steel wheel mounted at one end of a Japanned iron box. The method of using was to slide back the lid, exposing the tinder and draw a string wound on the spindle, thus rotating the wheel, which, coming in contact with a flint, caused a shower of sparks to fall within the box (332). This principle was also used for lighting purposes in mines containing explosive gases, the method being safe in such places. It was called a 'steel mill,' but was not much used as it gave a very poor light and was costly to run.

During the eighteenth century another expensive arrangement, called a 'pistol strike-a-light,' was brought out. The appearance and mechanism is very like a flint-lock pistol, the handle or butt, lock, trigger and pan being identical in every way. The pan holds the tinder, which becomes ignited when the hammer strikes and forces open the steel lid of the pan. They were made both for table and pocket use, the former being provided with short feet attached to the underside of the lock, and often a small candle socket at the side. A few examples are provided with a barrel, with a lid at the end; this acts as a match-box; others have a match-box fitted to the side.

The earlier type has the whole mechanism exposed (Fig. 334), later the springs were concealed inside the handle (333).

Another form of pistol strike-a-light is on the percussion-cap principle; but there are not many of these, as the introduction of the friction match rendered them obsolete soon after the idea originated.

Sulphur matches were usually kept within the tinder boxes, but a match holder for hanging upon a wall was made with a shaped iron plate against which the matches were held by two cords (Fig. 335). Containers for early-friction matches were of tinned iron, painted. The wall kind were fitted with a hinged lid and striking plate on the front (336). A common pocket variety held in addition to matches a candle and candle socket (337).

The candle box was common in every household during the eighteenth and nineteenth centuries. It was of sheet metal and hung on the wall horizontally. Some of the earlier examples are of brass, decorated by repoussé ornament (Fig. 338), but the usual type is of tinned iron painted or Japanned (339).

Two scissor-like implements were made in connection with the burning of candles; these were snuffers, known in parts of Scotland as candlesheres, the function of which was to trim the wick, and douters, or to give them their earlier name, out-quenchers, which were used as extinguishers. Of the two, snuffers are the earlier, and certainly date from the fifteenth century. In the *Privy Purse Expenses* of Henry VIII there are several references to them, for example:

'Item the same daye for vj payer of Snuffers ijs.'

During the early Stuart period their use had greatly increased, and the first year of Charles II saw an import duty of six shillings and eight pence on every dozen pairs. In the eighteenth century they became stereotyped, and formed part of the equipment of every household. They were rendered obsolete by a very simple invention—the introduction of a tight strand down one side of the plaited wick, which caused it to curl over into the outside of the flame where combustion was more rapid: this kept the wick at a short uniform length.

Snuffers were scissors with a box attached to hold the ends of the charred wicks. There was a considerable alteration in form during the long period of their usefulness. The earliest were of brass, iron, precious metal or metal and enamel, with a container on each blade, making a heart-shaped box when shut (Fig. 340). In the seventeenth century the double container was superseded by a single rectangular or semi-circular box, fitted to one blade, the other having a flat press which carried the cut wick into the box and extinguished it (342). A feature that is common to all periods is the spike which projects beyond the box; this was for uncurling the wick before cutting. Eighteenth-century snuffers were mostly made of steel, the later examples being highly burnished. The blades were held closed by a coil spring, concealed in the hinge (Fig. 343). These were made in various sizes, ranging from six to four and a half inches in length. The larger examples were supported upon three feet, one upon each handle bow and one under the box; the smaller upon one short foot under the box (344).

The chief difficulty with snuffers was that the short wick ends fell out as the blades opened. This fault brought about the introduction of a number of mechanical snuffers, the first being that of Benjamin Cartwright, a steel toy maker of the Strand, in 1749, who described his invention as 'a new kind of steel candle snuffers and stand, which by means of secret openings artfully disposed, make them by far the most curious, neat, and useful machine of the kind ever exhibited, and also the best calculated and contrived for preventing danger by fire, as they, by only opening them, cut off the snuff of the candle and retain so close that it can neither set fire to any thing by its scattering, nor be otherwise the least dangerous or offensive; also, by means of these secret springs, immediately discharge themselves without trouble or soiling the fingers, and their polish, which is exceeding bright and elegant, may be longer preserved than anything of this nature now in use, as they require little handling' (Fig. 347). Then in 1776 came Christopher Pinchbeck's patent which included 'Some simple additions to those very useful domestick machines called snuffers,' whereby the dropping of the wick is totally prevented. First improvement: 'A large recess or bottom' is fixed 'to the pan of the common snuffers,' a pressing plate 'is very nicely fitted in the pan' and comes 'quite flush to the front,' 'the bottom of the snuffers under the pan' is open 'the whole width of the pan' to let the wick fall into the recess and a narrow rim is soldered round the inside of the edge of the pan 'for the pressing plate to shut against and stop at.' Second improvement: The common pan is slit down at one-third of its depth from the front 'and a cutter acts on a centre fixed on a stud in front of the pan; it has a thumb piece at the other end to lift it up and down by, and when pushed down it goes behind a recess the thickness of a shilling made on the plate' (Fig. 351).

John Trusler, a clerk, brought out a similar invention in 1777. He maintained amongst other things that it 'entirely wipes or clears the inside of the cutter.' Next came John Wilks, a Sheffield gunsmith, who in 1801 constructed snuffers that had a cylinder upon which a door opened through the action of a rack and pinion (Fig. 352). In 1809, John Duff, a cutler of Great Pulteney Street, London, invented a mechanical snuffer which had in addition, on the point, 'two semi oval cuts, one plain, the other with a few sharp edges,' for the purpose of 'removing splinters or thieves in the wick of the candle' (Fig. 353). George Alexander Thompson, gentleman, the same year brought out an elaborate contrivance for 'cutting the wick of a lighted candle and keeping the same in perfect trim and of a proper length.' The peculiar feature in these snuffers is that they have twin cutting blades coming together from opposite sides.

Samuel Hobday, a snuffer maker of Birmingham, seems to have been the first to make a mechanical snuffer without springs. This he did in 1810 by having a concealed lever which worked by an eccentric on the hinge. This form of snuffer was produced by a number of different makers, whether by licence or not it is impossible to say. In 1811 Abraham Willis brought out a patent, which was followed by another from Hobday, who in 1818 invented a pair without any spring or levers (Fig. 348).

'On the short side of the snuffers are two ridges or inclined planes, one on the inner side to open the lid, and one on the outer side to shut it. The space between the inclined planes in shutting the snuffer prevents the action of the lid till the snuff is completely conveyed into the box and in opening till the cutting part of the snuffer blade is drawn from under it.'

One of the most remarkable patents was that of James Simpson, a surgical instrument maker of 55 Strand, who in 1820 brought out a somewhat elaborate arrangement which the following explanation, occurring in the abridged specification, may help to make clear:

'This improvement consists in the employment of compound levers by whose action a scraper is projected along the box and forces the snuff into a receptacle below. The levers are connected by pivot joints; they are attached at one extremity to the bows of the handles, and the other to the rod of the scraper. The receptacle is covered with a cap which is lifted by a lever. By bringing the bows together the 'moving chop' cuts the snuff off against the straight edge; the snuff immediately falls into 'the box' at the same (time) the levers project the scraper forward; this in its passage raises the 'lever' for the purpose of lifting the 'cap' and forces the snuff into the receptacle' (Fig. 349). Lee's patent, which followed in 1821, was provided with a false bottom which was prised up by an inclined plane attached to the inside of the cutter, the latter forming the lid of a small receptacle for retaining the snuff. In 1837 Henry N. S. Shrapnell of Bayswater Terrace thought of an entirely new method of retaining the snuff. In this invention the snuff is cut off in the common way by a cutting blade and press, and is then impaled upon a number of spikes fitted to the back of the container. The spikes can be removed for clearing purposes by unscrewing the back of the box (Fig. 355). Charles Greenaway, of Douglas, Isle of Man, invented snuffers in 1839 that had 'a well for receiving and securely retaining therein the candle snuff' (Fig. 354). Thomas W. Ingram's improvement was 'that in the art of cutting, one of the blades only with its handle shall be moveable, whilst the other blade with its handle remains relatively stationary' (Fig. 356). This was in 1841, and was followed the next year by two more. These were Septimus Cockings, a Birmingham draughtsman, and F. P. Walker, a Manchester coal merchant, whose invention consisted of a 'cutting part made long and convex' for the purpose of snuffing Walker's patent triple-wick candles (Fig. 357).

Two mechanical devices of which there seems to be no official record is Cope and Cutlers', with a circular container divided into two parts, the smaller having a vertical scraper which is projected rapidly forward as the press shuts; this causes the snuff to be thrown into the inner chamber. This large division is cleared out by lifting the lid (Fig. 350). The other has an inclined plane fitted to the top of the cutting blade: this lifts the shutter which snaps down when the snuffers close. To allow the cutting blade to open without lifting the shutter, the bottom of the shutter gives way in one direction only (Fig. 358).

In the living-rooms, snuffers were either placed upon trays or stands, the former being made in a variety of metals, though the shape was standardised as an oblong tray with the ends slightly raised (Fig. 361). These were in use from the beginning of the eighteenth century. Another less common design of cast brass has a carrying handle at the sides, the tray standing upon four short legs (362).

There are two principles of stands, one accommodating the snuffer vertically, the box fitting into a socket at the top of a stem (Fig. 359), and the other supporting them horizontally in two crutches; the latter were of steel richly ornamented by piercing (360).

Candles were extinguished in two ways, the most usual being by a metal cone often attached to candlesticks or snuffer stands, or by a douter, a similar implement to snuffers, but in place of a cutting blade and box it has two discs, between which the candle wick is nipped (Figs. 341 and 345). Some snuffers have douters attached to the end in place of the spike, but this was never a very common form (Fig. 346).

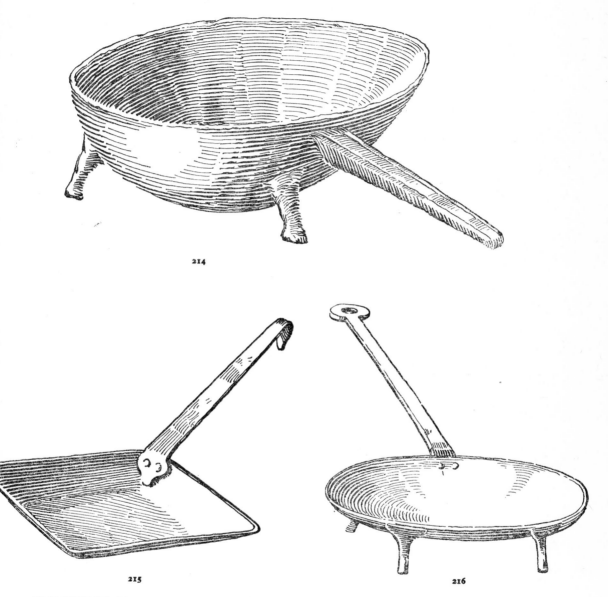

214

215                 216

214. GRISSETT IN CAST IRON, 17TH CENTURY, for melting tallow.   Length 11 ins.   *Author's collection*
215. GRISSETT IN SHEET IRON, 17TH–18TH CENTURY TYPE
216. GRISSETT IN CAST IRON, 17TH–18TH CENTURY TYPE

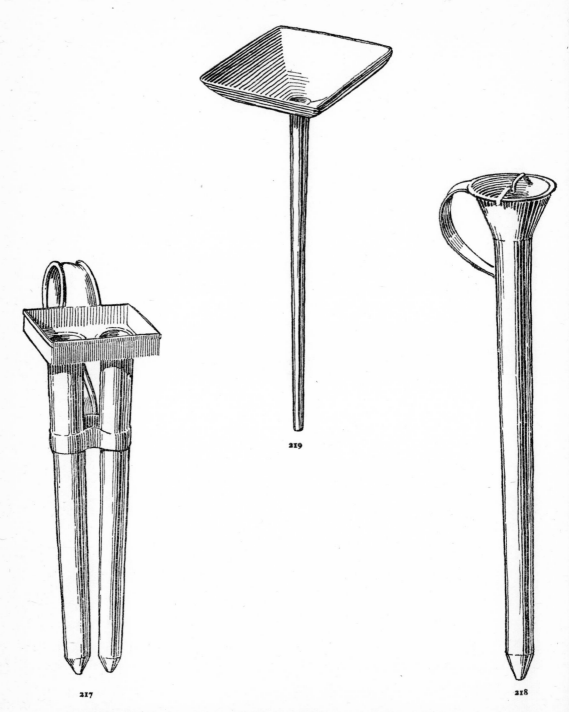

217. CANDLE MOULD, 18TH CENTURY. Length 11 ins. *Author's collection*
218. CANDLE MOULD, 18TH CENTURY. Length 13 ins. *Science Museum, South Kensington*
219. RUSHLIGHT DIPPER, 18TH CENTURY. *From Yorkshire*

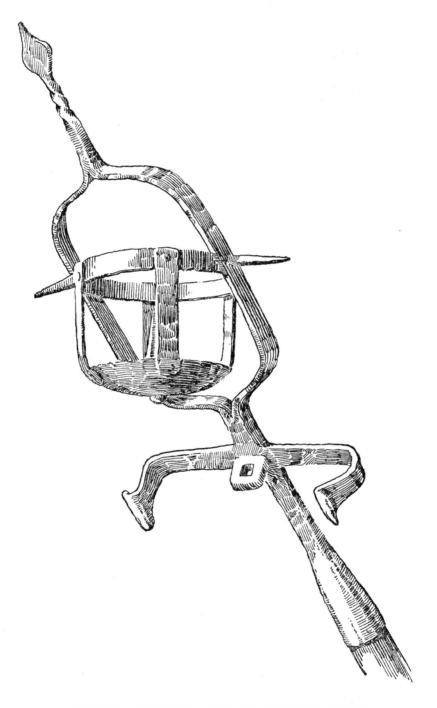

220. CRESSET, PORTABLE TYPE ON WOODEN STAFF
*John Lane collection*

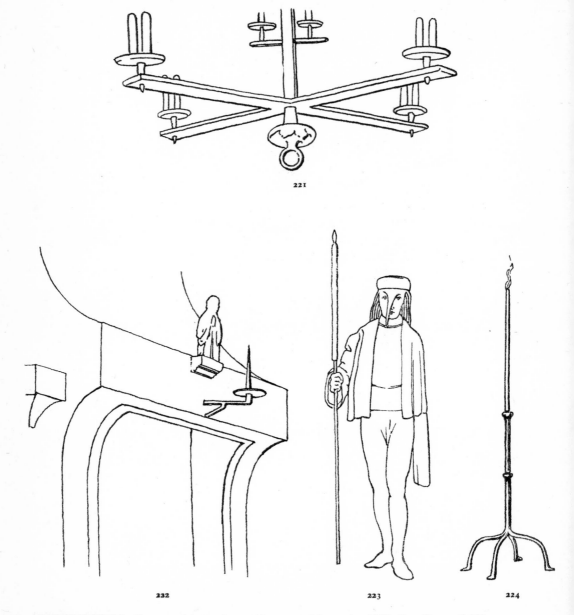

221

232                                                223                    224

221. CANDLE BEAM. *From a miniature in a 15th-century Manuscript (MS. Reg. E. 11, B.M.)*
222. PRICKET WALL BRACKET. *From a miniature in a 15th-century Manuscript (MS. Reg. E. 11, B.M.)*
223. CANDLE STAFF. *From a miniature in a 15th-century Manuscript (MS. Reg. E. 11, B.M.)*
224. CANDLE STANDARD IN IRON. *From a miniature in a Manuscript (MS. Egerton 2125, B.M.)*

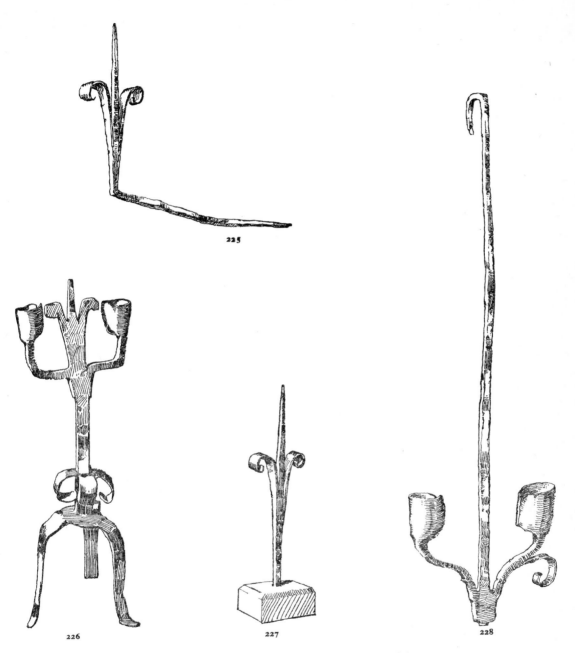

225. WALL PRICKET, 15TH AND 16TH CENTURY TYPE. Height 3¾ ins.
226. TABLE PRICKET AND CANDLESTICK, 15TH AND 16TH CENTURY TYPE. Height 7¼ ins.
227. TABLE PRICKET, 15TH AND 16TH CENTURY TYPE. Height 9 ins.
228. CANDLE PENDANT, 15TH AND 16TH CENTURY TYPE. Length 11½ ins.
*All from the Guildhall Museum*

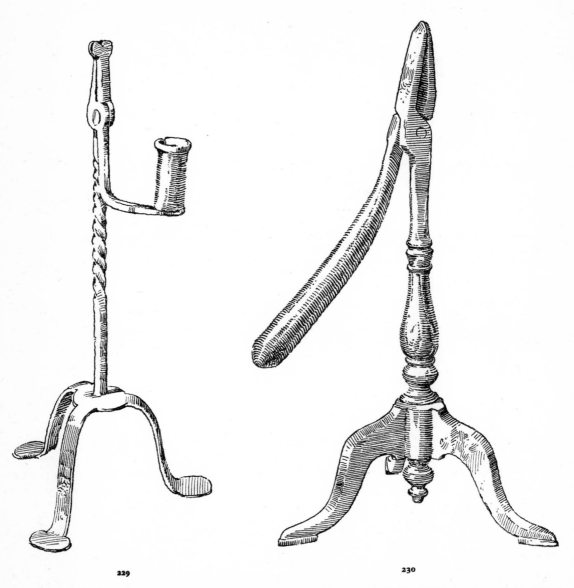

229

230

229. RUSH AND CANDLE HOLDER, WROUGHT IRON, 17TH CENTURY.  Height 11 ins.  *Colonel E. J. Harrison*

230. RUSH HOLDER, CAST IRON, LATE 18TH CENTURY TYPE.  Height 12 ins.  *Author's collection*

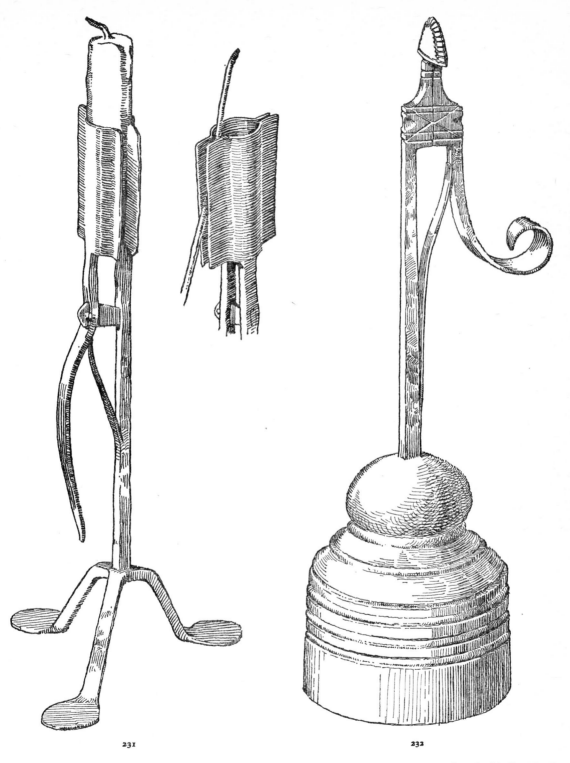

231                                                                              232

231. RUSH AND CANDLE HOLDER, LATE 17TH CENTURY. Height 8 ins. *Mr. C. M. Escaré*
232. RUSH HOLDER, 18TH CENTURY. Height 10 ins. *The Lady Carmichael*

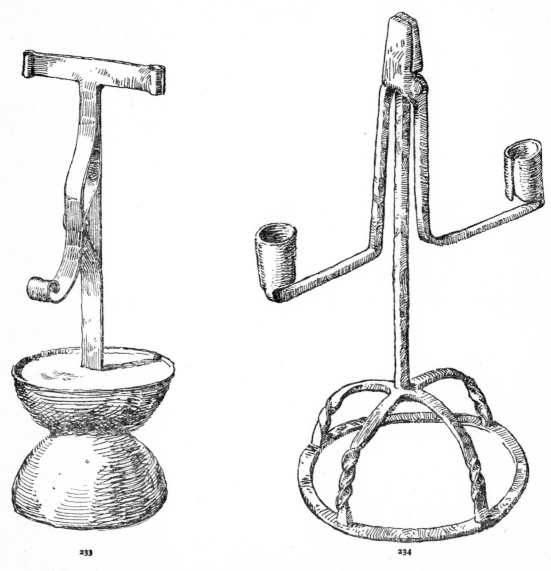

233. DOUBLE RUSHLIGHT HOLDER ON WOOD BASE. Height 7 ins. *Winchester Museum*
234. TWO-LIGHT CANDLE HOLDER AND RUSH CLIP, IRISH, 17TH CENTURY. Height 7 ins.

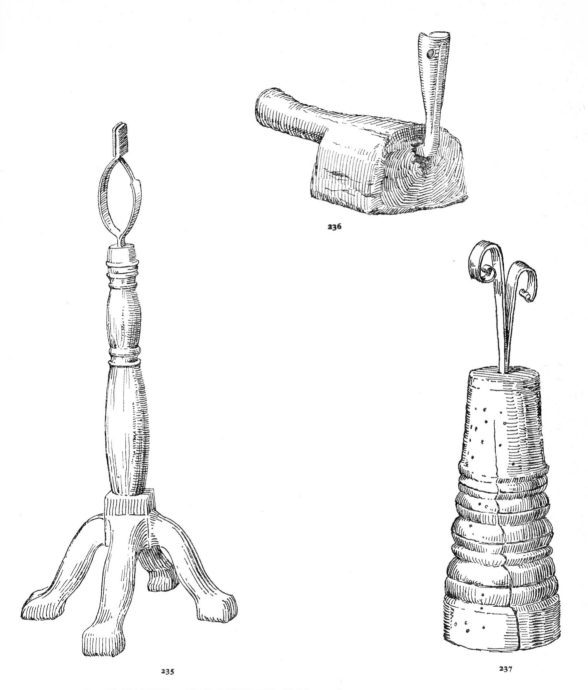

235. RUSH HOLDER, 18TH CENTURY. Height 11 ins.
236. RUSH AND CANDLE HOLDER, 18TH CENTURY. Height 4 ins. *Mr. Oswald Barron*
237. RUSH HOLDER, 18TH CENTURY. Height 9 ins. *Lewes Museum*

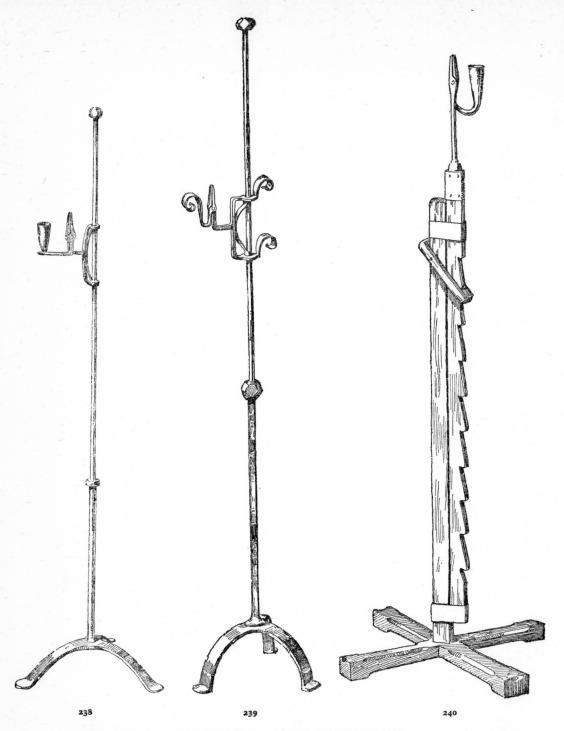

238                    239                    240

238. RUSH AND CANDLE HOLDER, 18TH CENTURY. Height 3 ft. 5 ins. *Lewes Museum*
239. RUSH HOLDER, 18TH CENTURY. Height 4 ft. *Lewes Museum*
240. RUSH HOLDER, 18TH CENTURY. Height 3 ft. 6 ins. *Victoria & Albert Museum*

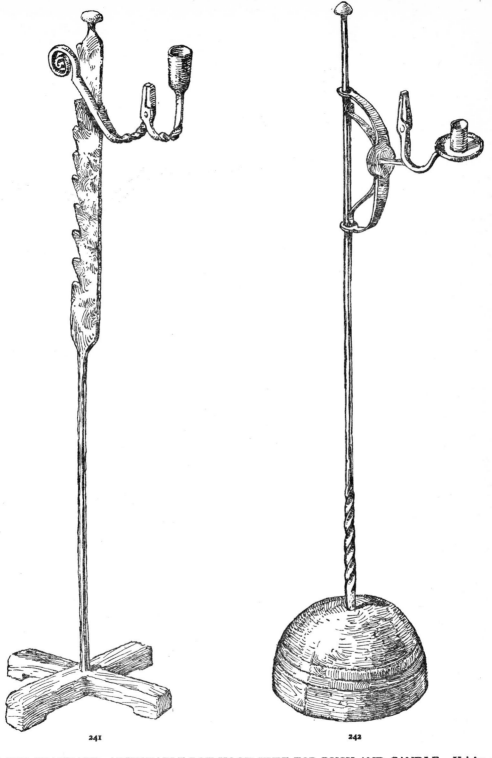

241. FLOOR STANDARD, ADJUSTABLE POT-HOOK TYPE FOR RUSH AND CANDLE.  Height 44 ins.
*From Boxgrove Priory, Sussex*
242. FLOOR STANDARD FOR RUSH AND CANDLE, MID 17TH CENTURY.  Height 54 ins. *From Ireland*

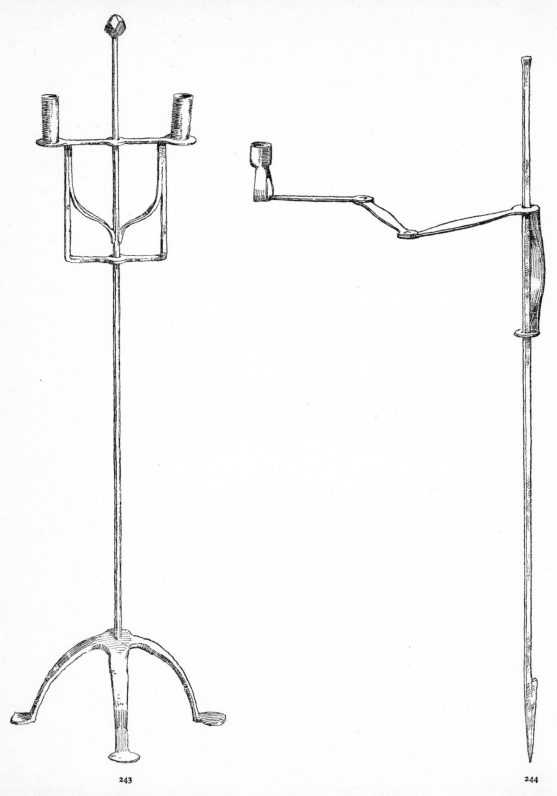

**243. CANDLE HOLDER, 18TH CENTURY.** Height 2 ft. 7 ins. (one leg missing). *The Geffrye Museum*
**244. CANDLE HOLDER, 18TH CENTURY.** Height 2 ft. 9 ins. *From Yorkshire*

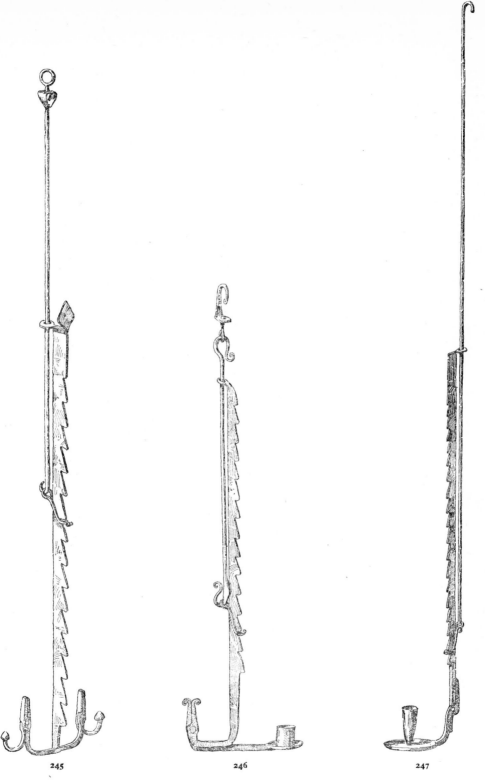

245. RUSH HOLDER, 18TH CENTURY.  Length 3 ft.  *The late Lady Dorothy Neville's collection*
246. RUSH AND CANDLE HOLDER, 18TH CENTURY.  Length 2 ft.  *The late Lady Dorothy Neville's collection*
247. RUSH AND CANDLE HOLDER, 18TH CENTURY.  Length 3 ft. 3 ins.  *Brighton Museum*

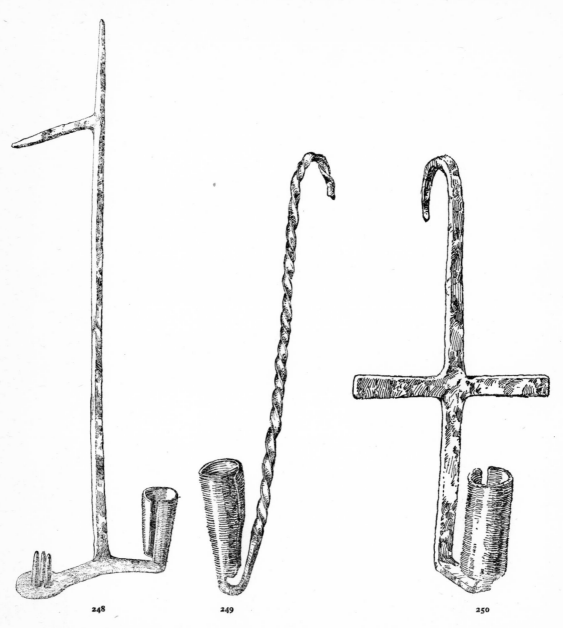

248. WROUGHT-IRON 'LUV' (Louvre) LIGHT from Gt. Yarmouth. Length overall 18 ins.
249. WROUGHT-IRON LOOM LIGHT from Belfast. Length overall 9¾ ins.
250. WROUGHT-IRON LOOM LIGHT from Belfast. Length overall 8 ins.

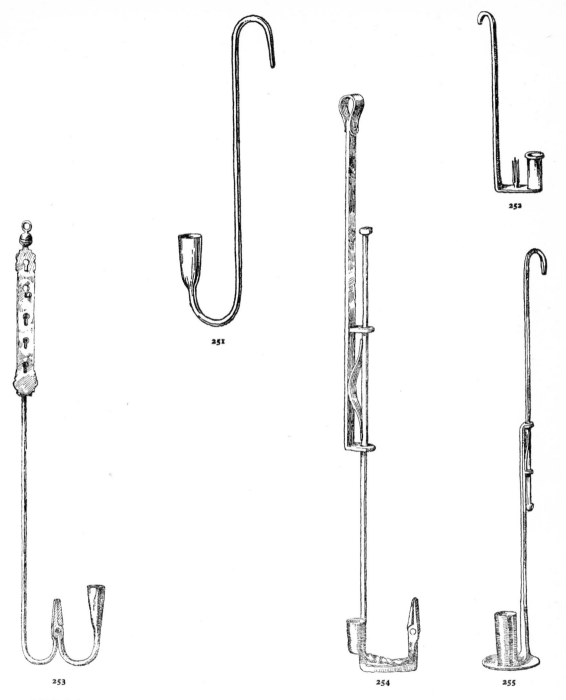

251. CANDLE HOLDER, 18TH CENTURY. Length 16 ins. *Victoria & Albert Museum*
252. CANDLE HOLDER, 18TH CENTURY. Length 9 ins. *Victoria & Albert Museum*
253. RUSH AND CANDLE HOLDER, 18TH CENTURY. Length 22 ins.
254. RUSH AND CANDLE HOLDER, 18TH CENTURY. Length 3 ft. *National Museum of Antiquities, Edinburgh*
255. CANDLE HOLDER, 18TH CENTURY. Length 21 ins. *National Museum of Antiquities, Edinburgh*

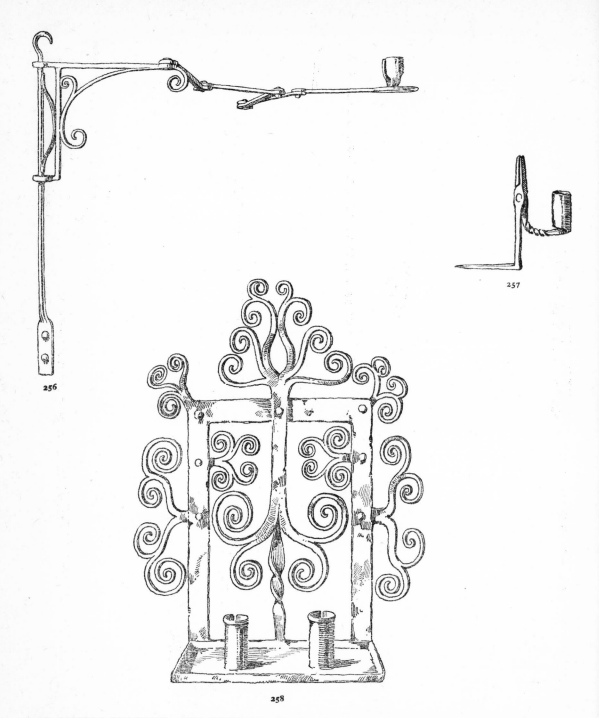

256. CANDLE BRACKET, 18TH CENTURY. Height 16½ ins. *National Museum of Antiquities, Edinburgh*
257. RUSH AND CANDLE BRACKET, 18TH CENTURY. Height 6 ins. *Victoria & Albert Museum*
258. CANDLE SCONCE, 18TH CENTURY. Height 18 ins. *Royal Scottish Museum, Edinburgh*

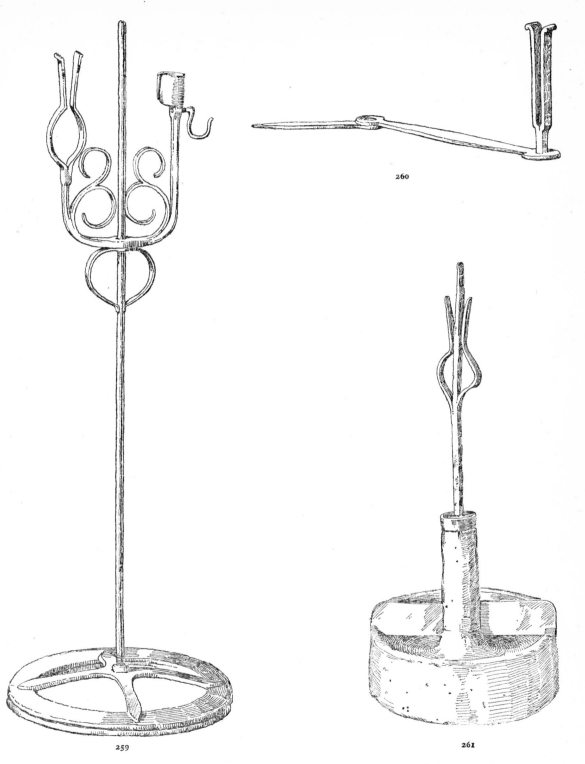

259. CANDLE-FIR AND CANDLE STANDARD, 18TH CENTURY. Height 23 ins.
260. WALL BRACKET FOR CANDLE-FIR, 18TH CENTURY. Height 3 ins.
261. CANDLE-FIR STANDARD, 18TH CENTURY. Height 15 ins.
*All from the National Museum of Antiquities, Edinburgh*

**263**

**264**

**265**

**262**

## BRASS CANDLESTICKS

262. 16TH CENTURY. Height 13½ ins. *British Museum*
263. 16TH CENTURY. Height 9 ins. *Mr. Oswald Barron*
264. 17TH CENTURY. Height 6 ins. *Victoria & Albert Museum*
265. 17TH CENTURY. Height 6 ins. *Guildhall Museum*

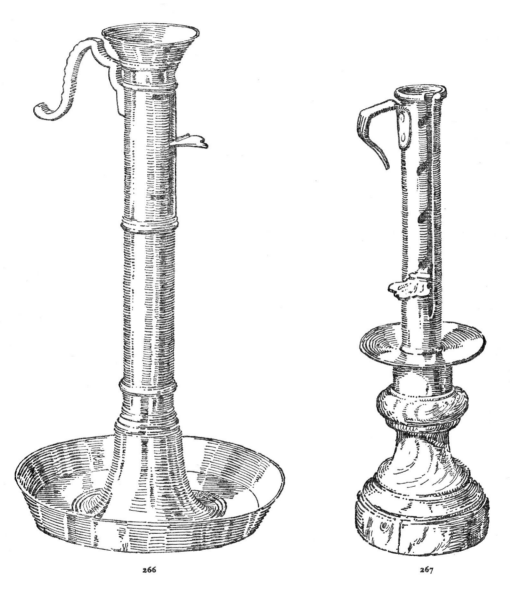

266. BRASS CANDLESTICK, EARLY 18TH CENTURY. Height 12¼ ins. *Mr. R. S. Williams*
267. BRASS AND WOOD CANDLESTICK, EARLY 18TH CENTURY. Height 11 ins. *Author's collection*

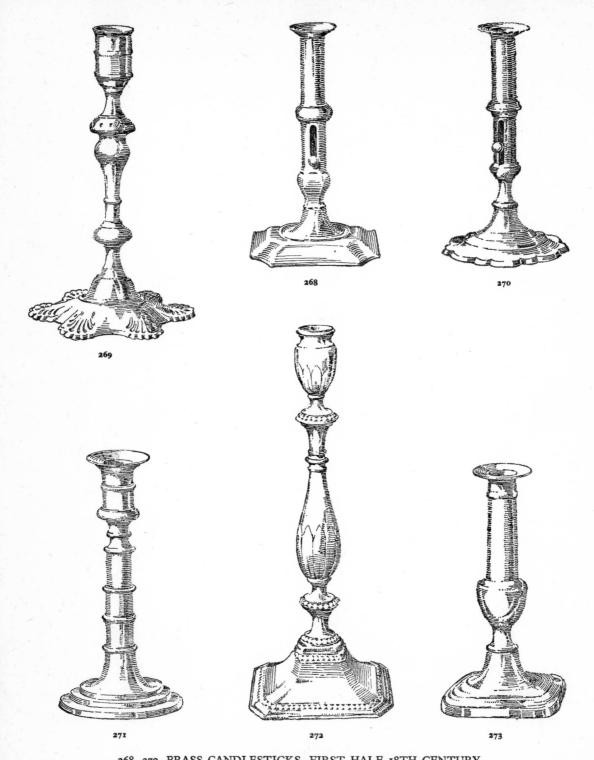

268, 270. BRASS CANDLESTICKS, FIRST HALF 18TH CENTURY
269. BRONZE CANDLESTICK, FIRST HALF 18TH CENTURY
271. BRASS CANDLESTICK, SECOND HALF 18TH CENTURY
272, 273. BRONZE CANDLESTICKS, SECOND HALF 18TH CENTURY
*All from the Author's collection*

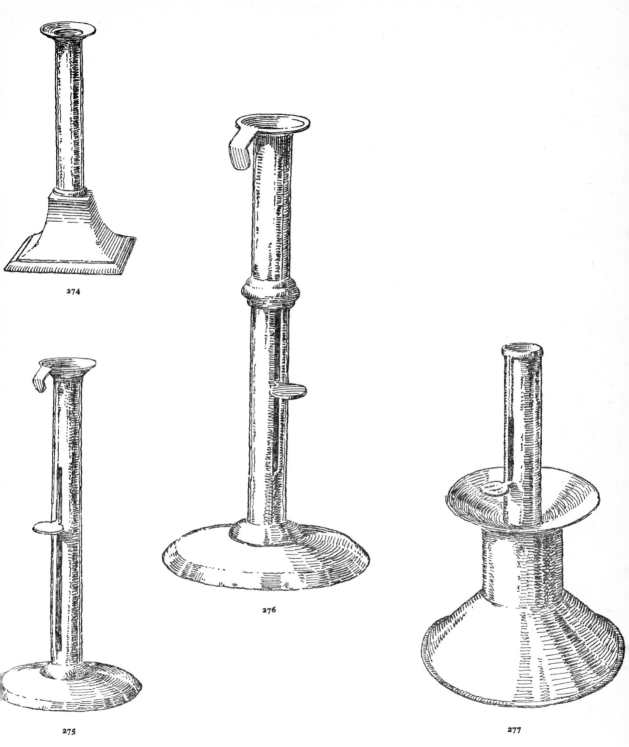

274. SHEET IRON CANDLESTICK WITH CAST-IRON BASE, EARLY 19TH CENTURY. *Author's collection*
275-277. SHEET IRON CANDLESTICKS, EARLY 19TH CENTURY. *Author's collection*

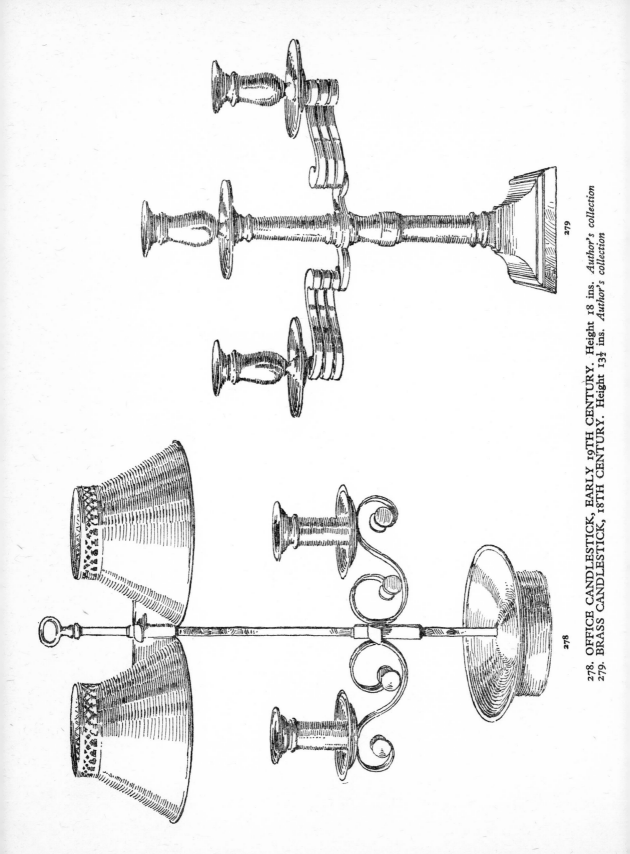

278. OFFICE CANDLESTICK, EARLY 19TH CENTURY. Height 18 ins. *Author's collection*
279. BRASS CANDLESTICK, 18TH CENTURY. Height 13¾ ins. *Author's collection*

278

279

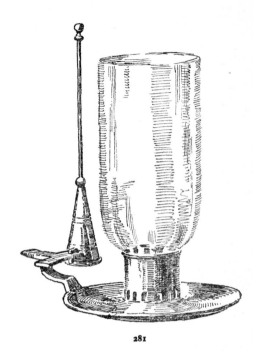

280

281

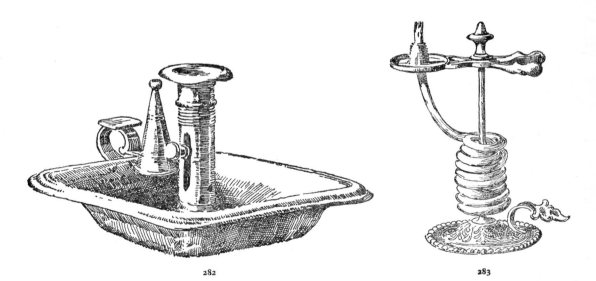

282

283

280, 282. BRASS BEDROOM CANDLESTICKS, LATE 18TH CENTURY. *Author's collection*
281. BRASS BEDROOM CANDLESTICK, EARLY 19TH CENTURY. *Mr. George Herbert*
283. BRASS TAPER HOLDER, LATE 18TH CENTURY. *Mrs. R. Russell*

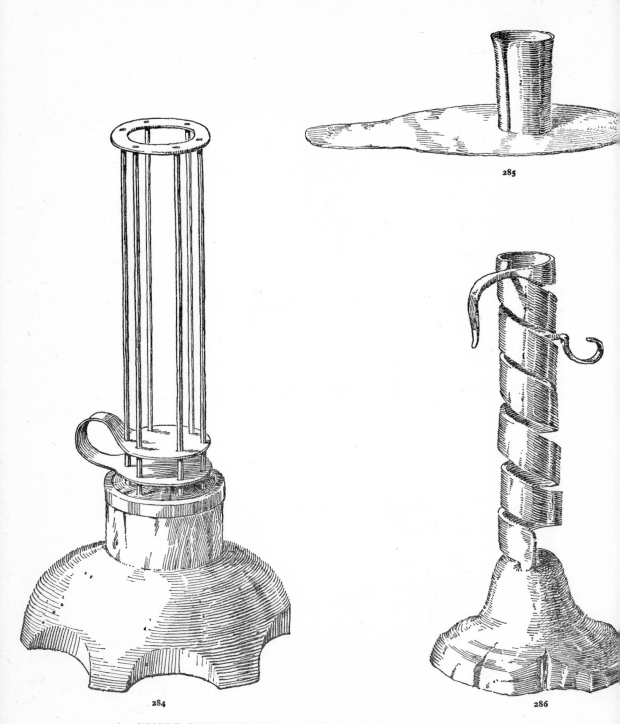

284. STABLE CANDLE HOLDER, 18TH CENTURY. Height 9 ins. *From Yorkshire*
285. CELLAR CANDLE HOLDER, 18TH CENTURY. *From Sussex*
286. CANDLESTICK ON WOOD BASE, 18TH CENTURY. *Mr. George Herbert*

**287. CANDELABRA OF BRASS**
The body dates from the late 15th century. The candle arms and busts early 17th century
*From St. Katherine's Hospital, Regent's Park*

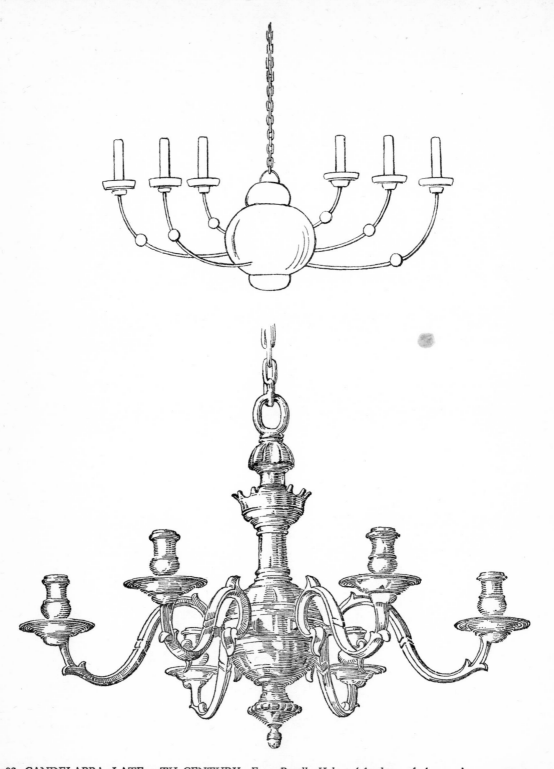

288. CANDELABRA, LATE 17TH CENTURY. *From Randle Holmes 'Academy of Armoury'*
289. CAST BRASS CANDELABRA, SHOWING RUSSIAN INFLUENCE, LATE 17TH CENTURY. Diameter 21 ins. *Mr. C. M. Escaré's collection*

290. CANDELABRA, WROUGHT-IRON, EARLY 17TH CENTURY. *Mr. I. C. Goodison*
291. CANDELABRA. Body of turned and carved wood, arms of wrought iron, candle sockets missing, late 18th century, from Scotland. *Author's collection*

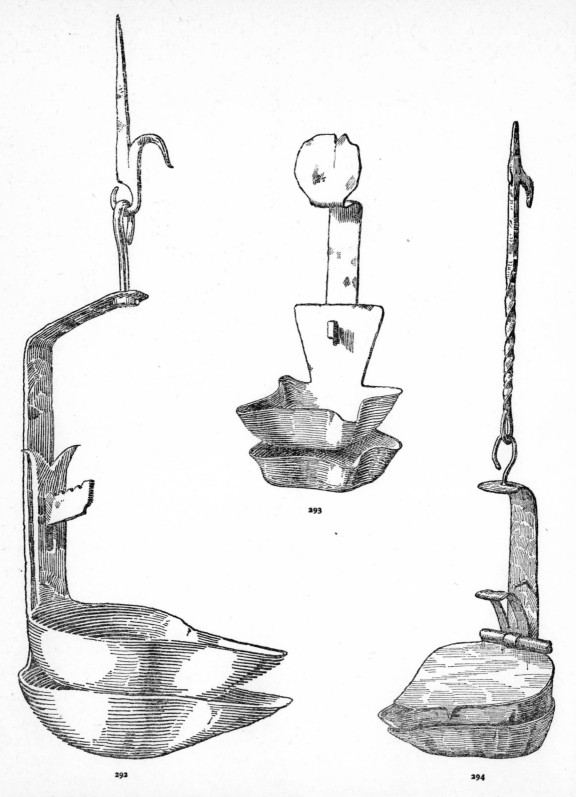

292. SCOTTISH LAMP ('CRUSIE'), WROUGHT-IRON, 17TH CENTURY. *Author's collection*
293. CORNISH LAMP ('CHILL'), COPPER, 17TH CENTURY. Suspension link missing. *From Cornwall*
294. CHANNEL ISLAND LAMP ('CRESSET'), WROUGHT-IRON, 17TH CENTURY. *Author's collection*

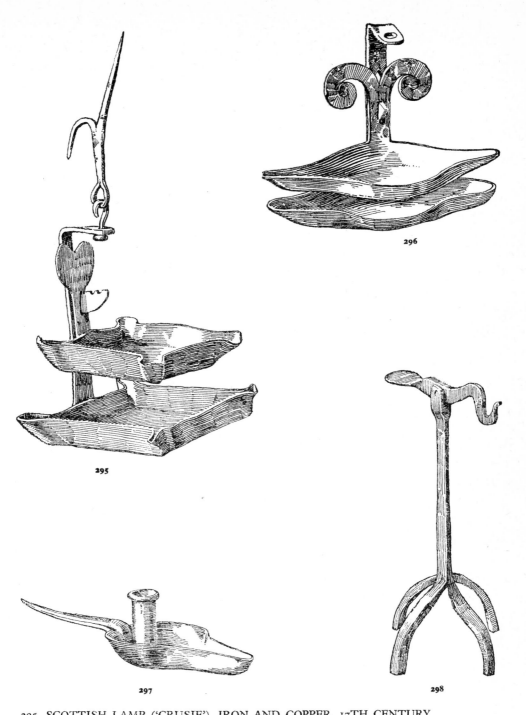

295. SCOTTISH LAMP ('CRUSIE'), IRON AND COPPER, 17TH CENTURY
296. SCOTTISH LAMP ('CRUSIE'), WROUGHT-IRON, 17TH CENTURY
297. SCOTTISH LAMP AND CANDLE HOLDER, WROUGHT-IRON, 18TH CENTURY
298. STAND FOR HOLDING CRUSIE LAMP, WROUGHT-IRON, 17TH CENTURY
*All from the National Museum of Antiquities, Edinburgh*

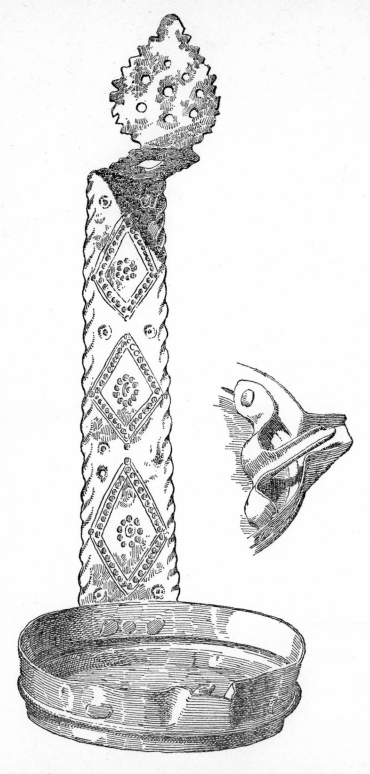

299. ENGLISH LAMP, REPOUSSÉ COPPER, 17TH CENTURY
Suspension link missing. Height 8½ ins. *Mr. H. W. Binns, F.S.I.*

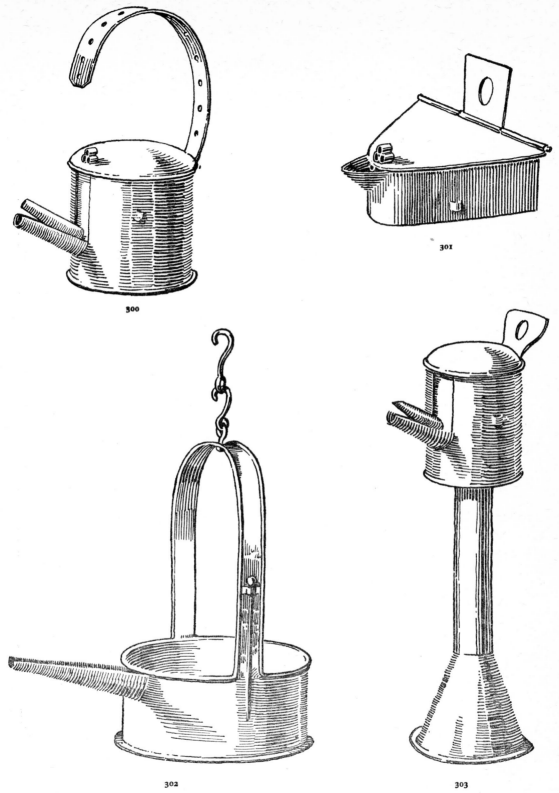

300. PENDANT SPOUT LAMP, TINNED IRON, 18TH CENTURY. *Late Lady Dorothy Neville*
301. WALL LAMP, TINNED IRON, 18TH CENTURY. *Late Lady Dorothy Neville*
302. PENDANT LAMP, TINNED IRON, 18TH CENTURY. *From the Channel Islands*
303. TABLE LAMP, TINNED IRON, 18TH CENTURY. *Late Lady Dorothy Neville*

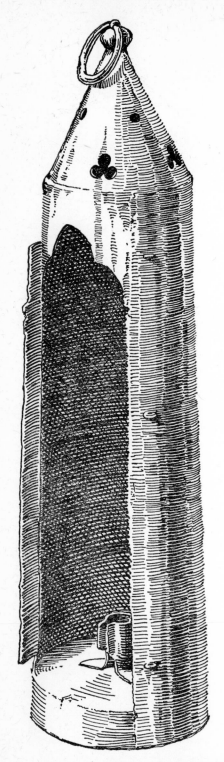
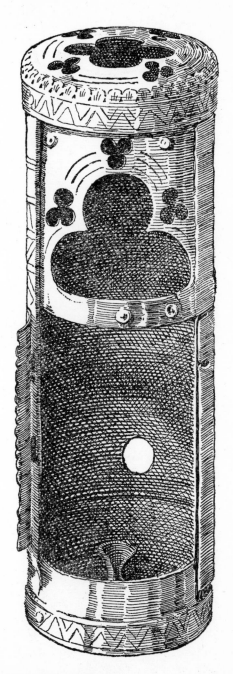

**304, 305. BRONZE HAND LANTERNS, 14TH–15TH CENTURY**
*The London Museum*

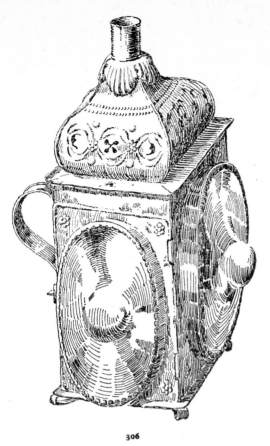

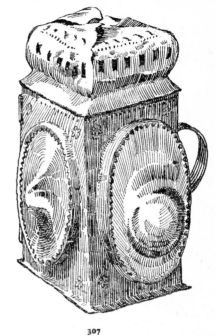

306

307

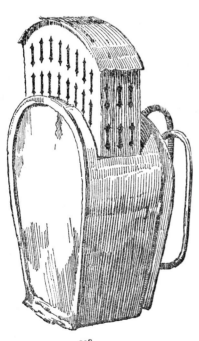

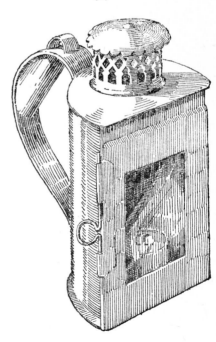

308

309

## HAND LANTERNS

306. SHEET BRASS, LATE 17TH CENTURY. *Gas Light & Coke Co.*
307. SHEET BRASS, LATE 17TH CENTURY. *National Museum of Antiquities, Edinburgh*
308. SHEET COPPER, EARLY 19TH CENTURY. *National Museum of Antiquities, Edinburgh*
309. JAPANNED IRON, MID 19TH CENTURY. *Gas Light & Coke Co.*

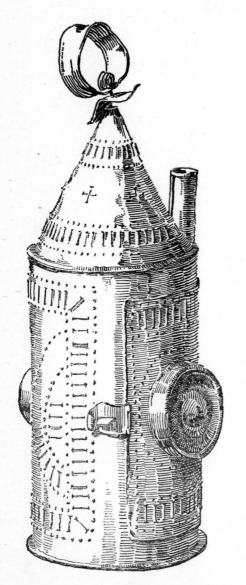

310. HAND LANTERN, TINNED IRON, EARLY 18TH CENTURY
311. HAND LANTERN, SHEET BRASS, DATED 1750
*Both from National Museum of Antiquities, Edinburgh*

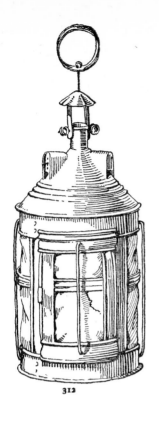

312

313

314

315

HAND LANTERNS, EARLY 19TH CENTURY
312. SHEET IRON, HORN PANELS          313. SHEET IRON, GLASS PANELS
314. SHEET IRON, GLASS CYLINDER       312–314. *From Author's collection*
315. SHEET IRON, PERFORATED CYLINDER. *Brighton Museum*

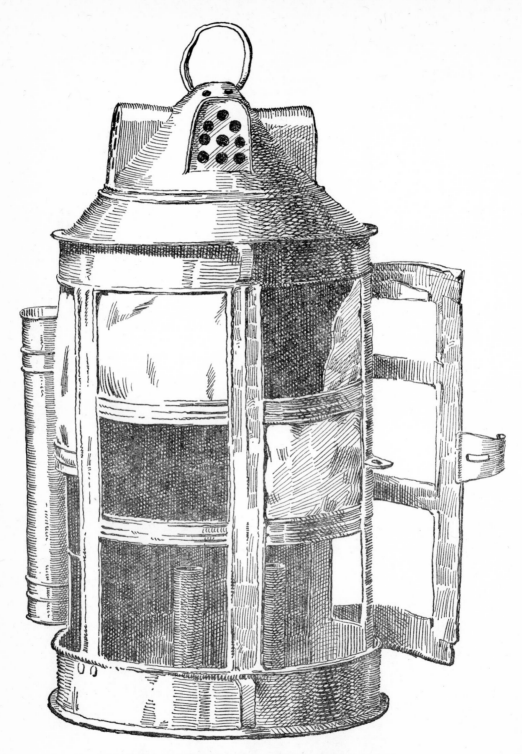

316. WAGON LANTERN, SHEET IRON, EARLY 19TH CENTURY
Height 24 ins. *Brighton Museum*

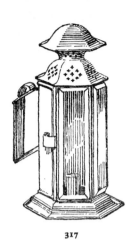

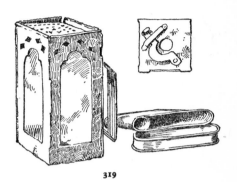

317

318

319

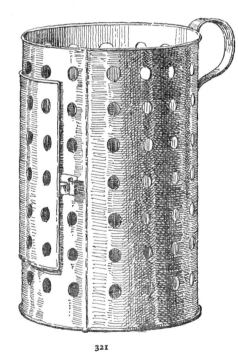

320

321

322

317. HAND LANTERN, SHEET IRON, PAINTED, EARLY 19TH CENTURY. *Author's collection*
318. WALL LANTERN, SHEET IRON, PAINTED, EARLY 19TH CENTURY. *Victoria & Albert Museum*
319. FOLDING POCKET LANTERN, SHEET IRON, EARLY 19TH CENTURY. *Geffrye Museum*
320. HAND LANTERN, WIRE GAUZE AND SHEET IRON, EARLY 19TH CENTURY. *Author's collection*
321. CANDLE SCREEN, JAPANNED IRON, EARLY 19TH CENTURY. *Author's collection*
322. HAND LANTERN, PERFORATED IRON, EARLY 19TH CENTURY. *Brighton Museum*

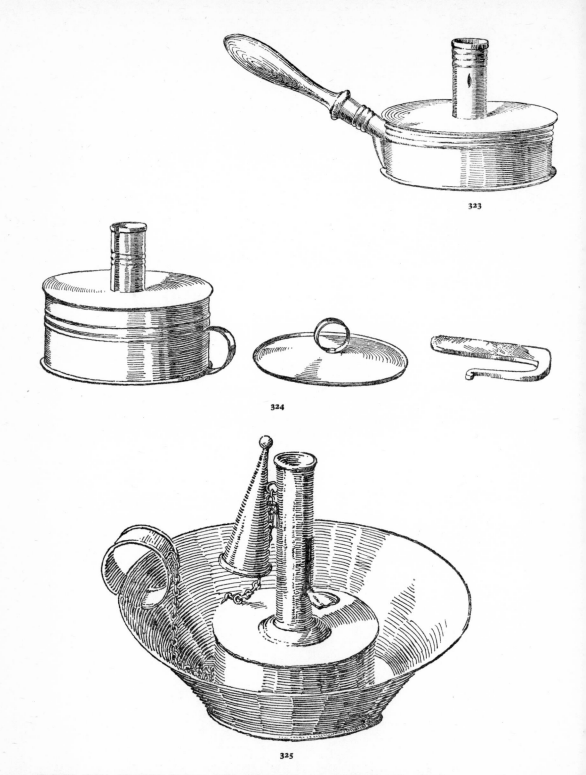

323. TINDER BOX, TINNED IRON, 18TH CENTURY. *Mr. C. M. Escaré's collection*
324. TINDER BOX, TINNED IRON, 18TH CENTURY. *Author's collection*
325. TINDER BOX AND CANDLESTICK, TINNED IRON, EARLY 19TH CENTURY. *Bryant & May's Museum*

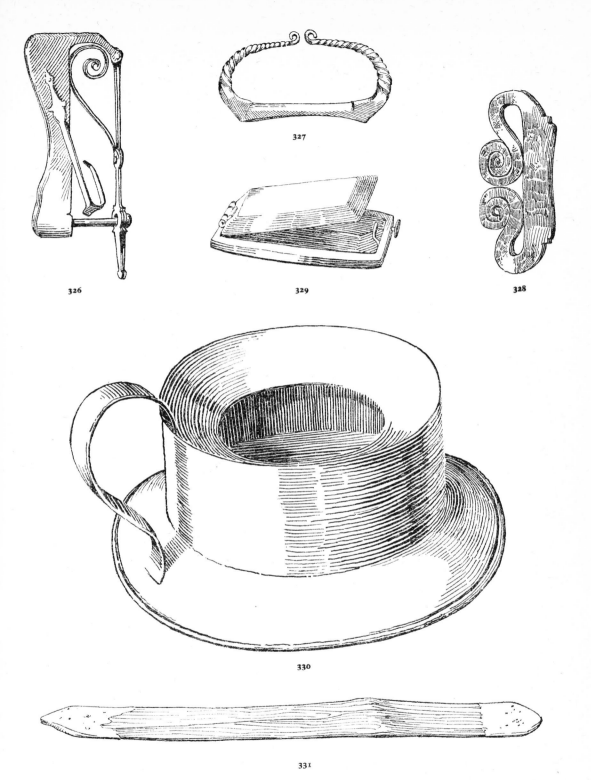

326. COMBINED STEEL AND TINDER TONGS, 18TH CENTURY. *Victoria & Albert Museum*
327. STEEL, 18TH CENTURY, from Edinburgh. *Author's collection*
328. STEEL, 18TH CENTURY. *Author's collection*
329. POCKET TINDER BOX, 18TH CENTURY. *Author's collection*
330. RECEPTACLE FOR MELTING SULPHUR, TINNED IRON, EARLY 19TH CENTURY. *Lewes Museum*
331. SULPHUR MATCH (SPUNK). *Author's collection*

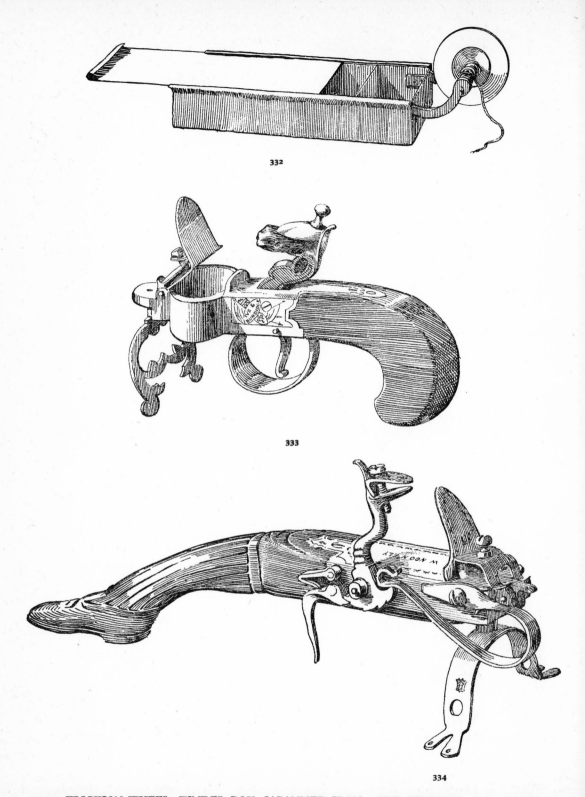

332. FRICTION WHEEL, TINDER BOX, JAPANNED IRON, 18TH CENTURY. *Lewes Museum*
333. FLINTLOCK TINDER BOX, LATE 18TH CENTURY. *Brighton Museum*
334. FLINTLOCK TINDER BOX, EARLY 18TH CENTURY. *Mr. C. M. Escaré's collection*

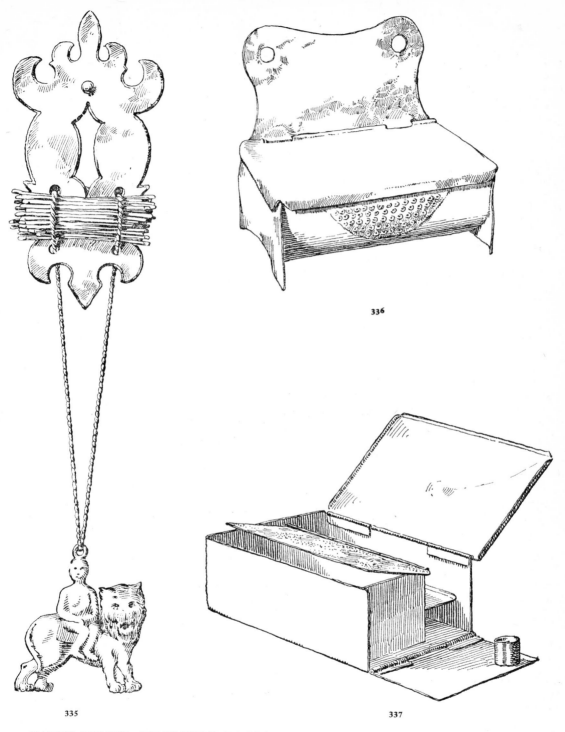

335. MATCH HOLDER, WROUGHT-IRON PLATE AND LEAD WEIGHT, LATE 18TH CENTURY.
  From York
336. MATCH BOX, PAINTED IRON, MID 19TH CENTURY. *Author's collection*
337. MATCH AND CANDLE BOX, MID 19TH CENTURY. *Author's collection*

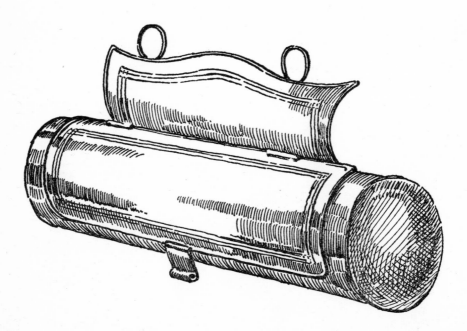

338. CANDLE BOX, BRASS REPOUSSÉ, LATE 17TH CENTURY.  Length 12 ins. *Mr. Ralph Edwards*
339. CANDLE BOX, JAPANNED IRON, LATE 19TH CENTURY.  Length 14 ins. *The late L. G. Russell-Davies bequest*

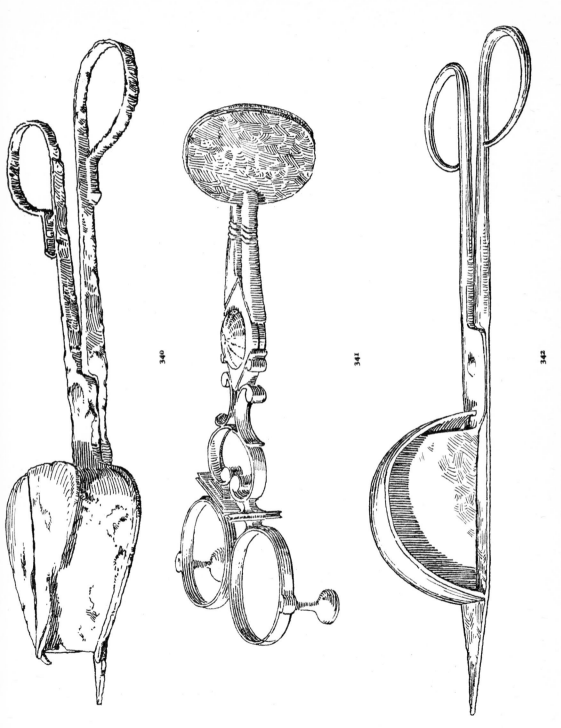

340. SNUFFERS, WROUGHT IRON, EARLY 17TH CENTURY
341. DOUTERS, WROUGHT IRON, EARLY 18TH CENTURY
342. SNUFFERS, WROUGHT IRON, EARLY 18TH CENTURY
*All from the Author's collection*

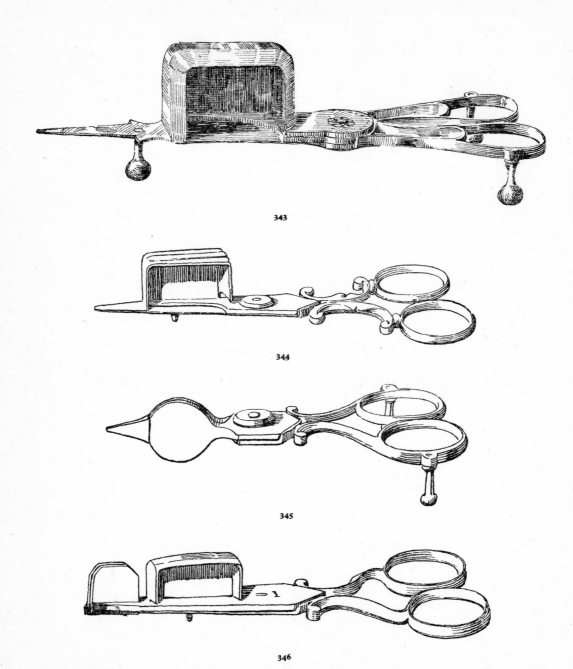

343. SNUFFERS, WROUGHT STEEL, LATE 18TH CENTURY
344. SNUFFERS, WROUGHT STEEL, LATE 18TH CENTURY
345. DOUTERS, WROUGHT STEEL, LATE 18TH CENTURY
346. COMBINED SNUFFERS AND DOUTER, WROUGHT STEEL, LATE 18TH CENTURY
*All from the Author's collection*

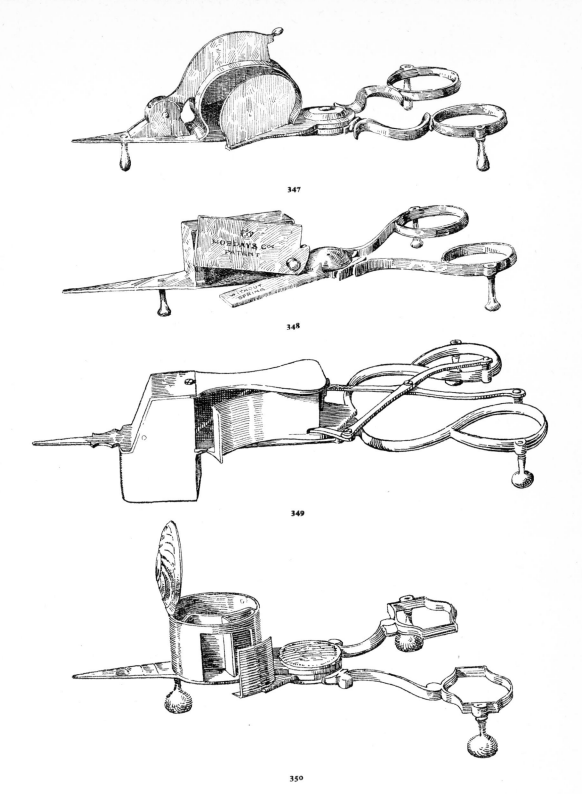

347-349. MECHANICAL SNUFFERS, LATE 18TH AND EARLY 19TH CENTURY. *Author's collection*
350. MECHANICAL SNUFFER, EARLY 19TH CENTURY. *Gas Light & Coke Co.*

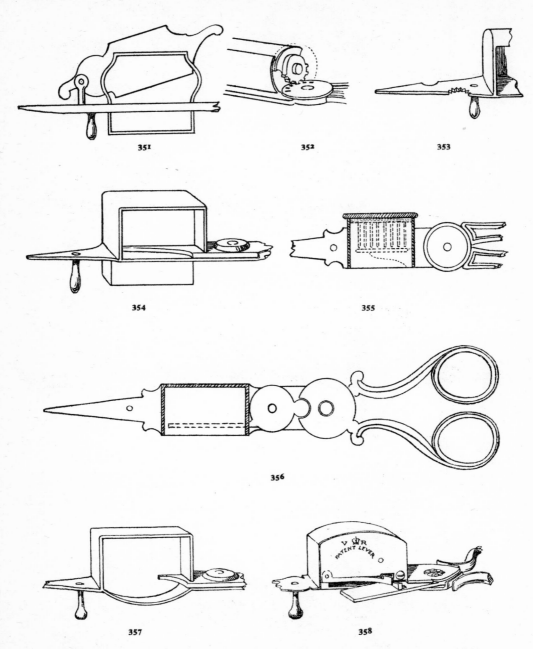

351                    352                    353

354                              355

356

357                              358

351–358. MECHANICAL SNUFFER MOVEMENTS, 18TH AND 19TH CENTURY

359. BRASS SNUFFERS AND STAND, MIDDLE 18TH CENTURY. *Croft-Lyons bequest*
360. PIERCED STEEL SNUFFER STAND, LATE 18TH CENTURY. *Victoria & Albert Museum*
361. JAPANNED IRON SNUFFER TRAY, LATE 18TH CENTURY. *Author's collection*
362. CAST-BRASS SNUFFER TRAY, LATE 18TH CENTURY. *Victoria & Albert Museum*

PART FOUR

# TOBACCO SMOKING

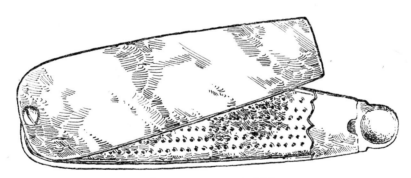

SNUFF RASP, 18TH CENTURY

PART FOUR

# TOBACCO SMOKING

TOBACCO IS SAID TO have been first introduced into Europe in the year 1560 by Franceso Hernandez, a Spanish physician, who obtained it in Mexico. It was introduced into France about the same time by the then French Ambassador to the Portuguese Court, Jean Nicot, who purchased some Florida tobacco from a Flemish merchant and sent it to the Grand Prior of France; which accounts for it first being called *Herbe du Grand Prieur*. The name was shortly after altered to *Herbe de la Reine* and *Herbe Medicee*, in compliment to the French Queen. The native name of Petun was also occasionally used. All these terms were dropped for the name Nicotina, which was evolved from the name of the original importer, Nicot. The name Nicotina eventually gave way to the more general term *tabac*, the French equivalent to our word tobacco, the name by which the herb has been known in England from the beginning of the seventeenth century.

The tobacco plant came to Europe through Spain, but the habit of smoking the leaf was spread through English example. It is generally accepted that Ralph Lane, first Governor of Virginia, and Sir Francis Drake brought back with them tobacco and pipes which they handed to Sir Walter Raleigh, who caused it to become a vogue among young men who could afford it. Many amusing incidents must have arisen before the novelty wore off; there is a familiar one connected with Sir Walter Raleigh, but another somewhat similar, and rendered all the more curious by its Welsh phrasing, is told by Barnaby Rich in his *Irish Hubbub* (1619), and is as follows: 'I remember a pretty jest of tobacco which was this. A certain Welshman coming newly to London and beholding one to take tobacco, never seeing the like before, and not knowing the manner of it, but perceiving him vent smoke so fast and supposing his inside parts to be on fire, cried out, "O Jhesu, Jhesu man, for the passion of God hold, for by God's splud ty snout's on fire;" and having a bowl of bere in his hand, threw it at the other's face to quench his smoking nose.'

The habit grew apace, and for various reasons, partly because of its soothing influence, partly because it was the 'correct thing,' and again because it was supposed to have wonderful medicinal properties. And as the habit spread, not only in England but practically over the whole of Europe, there grew a strong opposition to its use. Headed by James I, who in 1604 published his famous *Counterblast to Tobacco*, England was followed by other countries; in Russia persons convicted of smoking had the nose amputated; in the Canton of Berne in Switzerland, it was ranked as an offence next to adultery; Urban VIII, in 1624, excommunicated all who used tobacco in Church, and Innocent XII, in 1690, did the same; Amurath IV of Turkey used to suppress it by torture.

The *Counterblast to Tobacco* is ample evidence that James I detested the chewing and smoking or drinking, as it was then commonly called, of tobacco. Regarding the extravagance of the habit, he says: 'Now how you are by the custom disabled in your goods, let the gentry of this land bear witness; some of them bestowing three, some four hundred pounds a year upon this precious stink.' He sums it up as 'A custom loathsome to the eye, hateful to the nose, harmful to the brain, dangerous to the lungs, and in the black stinking fumes thereof nearest resembling the horrible Stygian smoke of the pit that is bottomless.'

Robert Burton, in his *Anatomy of Melancholy* (1652), speaks most emphatically against the habit as commonly indulged in: 'Tobacco, divine, rare, and super-excellent tobacco, which goes far beyond all the panaceas, potable gold, and philosophers' stones, the sovereign remedy for all deseases. A good vomit, I confess, a virtuous herb, if it be well qualified, opportunely taken, and medicinally used; but as it is commonly abused by most men, which take it as tinkers do ale, 'tis a plague, a mischief, a violent purger of goods, lands, health, hellish, devilish and damned tobacco, the ruin and overthrow of body and sole.'

Many methods were adopted to check the growth of the habit. In the reign of James I some Justices of the Peace for Kent issued a licence to an alehouse in which the following clause appears: 'You shall not utter nor willingly suffer to be uttered, drunke, or taken, any tobacco within your house, cellar or other place thereunto belonging.' The clergy took a strong stand against the use of tobacco and preached sermons condemning it.

In the House of Commons on Wednesday, 16 April 1621, Sir William Stroud moved that he 'Would have tobacco banished wholly out of the Kingdom, and that it may not be brought in from any part, nor used amongst us;' and Sir Grey Palmer said, 'that if tobacco be not banished it will overthrow one hundred thousand men in England, for now it is so common that he hath seen ploughmen take it as they are at Plough.'

Two years before this, in 1619, Barnaby Rich made his strong attack against this 'Filthy Antidote.' He says: 'Oh base conditional time, is wit so far spent amongst Knights and Gentlemen, that they can employ no better indeavours, but to imitate that abuse which is so common to every Ostler, with every Tapster, with every Tinker, with every Costermonger, with every Horse boy and to conclude, that is such use and custom with every rogue and rascal.' And again: 'They say that Welshmen came running out of Heaven, when they heard one without the Gate, crying Canse Bobby, Canse Bobby (Toasted cheese); but I think an Englishman would run as fast into Hell, if they did but hear a voice crying out—a pipe of Tobacco.'

The hostility against smoking was long lived, in spite of the rapid growth of the habit, and we find in the Minutes of the Friends' Monthly Meeting at Penketh, Lancashire, the following entry:

'14th, 4th mo. 1691—It being considered that the too frequent use of smoking tobacco is inconsistent with Friends holy profession, it is desired that such as have occasion to make use thereof take it privately, neither too publickly in their own house, nor by the high ways, streets, nor in alehouses, or elsewhere, tending to the abetting the common excess.

'18th, 8th mo. 1691—Friends not to smoke during their labour or occupation but to leave their work and take it privately.'

The foregoing extracts show that tobacco smoking had its opponents; but it also had, in a much larger degree, its champions and adherents.

Among the earliest smokers in this country was the notorious Sir Edward Darrell. An entry in the accounts of his household shows that he bought pipes and tobacco in 1589, only three years after its introduction. From this time down to the end of the eighteenth century, when it was banished, tobacco was successfully cultivated in England, although the amount under cultivation varied considerably. It was prohibited by James I and Charles I, and also during the Commonwealth in 1652. Christopher Wilkenson states in a pamphlet published in 1682 that: 'It is planted in great plenty in Gloucester, Devonshire, and in several gardens about Westminster and other parts of Middlesex,' and that, 'His Majesty sending every year a troop of horse to destroy it lest the trade of our American plantations should be incommoded thereby.'

It is quite certain that very many people during the seventeenth century had great faith in it as a cure, or preservative against disease. Rich in his *Irish Hubbub* (1619) says: 'There is no man that doth use to take Tobacco, but he must take upon him the imputation of some disease or else he must acknowledge himself to be a foole.' In the *Reliquiæ Hearnianæ*, edited by Dr. Philip Bliss, there is the following entry, 1720–1721, January 21: 'I have been told that in the last great plague in London (i.e. 1665) none that had tobaconist's shops had the plague. It is certain, that smoking it was looked upon as a most excellent preservative. In so much that even children were obliged to smoke. And I remember that I heard formerly, Tom Rogers, who was yeoman beadle say, that where he was that year, when the plague raged, a schoolboy at Eton, all the boys of that school were obliged to smoak in school every morning, and that he never was whipped so much in his life as he was one morning for not smoking.'

There was a fair amount of literature of a sort in praise of tobacco. The following is from a volume of songs, *Le Prince d'Amour*, etc., published in 1660 by William Leake.

A SONG IN PRAISE OF TOBACCO

To feed on flesh is gluttoning
    It maketh men fat like swine;
But is not he a frugal man
    That on a leaf can dine?
He needs no linnen for to foul
    His fingers' ends to wipe
That has his kitchen in a box
    And roast meat in a pipe.
The cause wherefore few rich men's sons
    Prove disputants in schools,
Is that their fathers fed on flesh
    And they begat fat fools.
This fulsome feeding cloggs the brain
    And doth the stomach choak
But he's a brave spark that can dine
    With one light dish of smoak.

The cost of tobacco in 1589, three years after it was first introduced into this country, was five shillings the ounce. This was not a fixed rate, as in the same accounts there is an item, 'half a pound of tobacco thirty shillings,' making the ounce cost three shillings and ninepence.

The duty about this time was twopence per pound; this was raised to six shillings and tenpence by Act of Parliament by James I. In 1611, 'a pipe of rich smoke was sold for 6d.' That the price must have fallen considerably soon after this is evident from Rich saying, in 1619, that smoking was 'an abuse which is so common with every ostler, tinker, etc.,' and from Sir Grey Palmer's observation, two years later, that 'he has seen ploughmen take it as they are at Plough.' During the latter half of the seventeenth century the price had greatly fallen, an entry in the Journal of the Rev. Thomas Moore of Horstead Keynes reading, '2 oz. tobacco 1/-.'

Metal objects, owing their origin exclusively to the use of tobacco, are not to be found in great variety, but are none the less interesting, and show in their manufacture much ingenuity and fine workmanship; especially does this apply to pipe tongs. These articles probably began to appear about the beginning of the seventeenth century. Pipe tongs were also known as ember tongs, tobacco tongs, smokers' tongs. They are of two distinct types—the larger examples used to secure an ember from the fire, and the small pocket tongs for taking up smouldering tinder. The former were made in wrought iron or steel (Figs. 363 to 365). The jaws are kept together by a spring fitted between the handles, most examples having a tobacco stopper fixed at the side which is an elongation of the hinge-pin and another of larger diameter at the end of one or both handles (363 and 365).

A very fine example in wrought iron with openwork handles, the ends of which are finished off as tobacco stoppers, one of which unscrews and forms a pricker for unstopping a pipe bowl, is in the Guildhall Museum (364). These tongs were very personal possessions, and often bore the owner's initials. They were more delicate than fire tongs, and usually ornamented by chamfering. There are a number of pipe tongs in public and private collections throughout the country, showing that they must have been in general use during the eighteenth and nineteenth centuries. Some examples have a whistle at the end of one handle, and were for use in Inns; this whistle enabled a customer, who might be enjoying the seclusion of the inglenook, to call the attention of the bar attendant. The small type were not so common, and were more varied in design. They were made in steel and brass, with and without springs. A late seventeenth century brass example in the Guildhall Museum shows a carefully considered scheme of chamfering, and has a tobacco stopper at the end of one of the handles (Fig. 366).

Another brass pair of the same period are in the form of miniature fire tongs. These were dug up on the site of the late Royal Aquarium (368). In steel they are made on similar lines to the large ember tongs with spring and tobacco stopper (367), and also in the form of tweezers, the handle forming the tobacco stopper (369).

There are two kinds of metal tobacco box, those of a convenient size and weight for the pocket, and those for table use, the prototype of the modern tobacco jar; the latter were made in lead painted, and, in lesser numbers, in cast iron, pewter and brass (Figs. 370 to 373). Inside was a press which kept the tobacco compact and free from air. Two pocket boxes are shown in Figs. 374 and 375, the latter being decorated with stamped ornament. Tobacco boxes were also made in the middle of the nineteenth century in conjunction with a pipe case (Fig. 386). The reason why portable tobacco boxes of an ornamental character are not common is that the use of tobacco out of doors was not considered correct for a gentleman until quite recently. Had this not been so, tobacco boxes would probably have been as plentiful and varied as snuff boxes.

Tobacco stoppers were made in great numbers during the seventeenth and eighteenth centuries; by the middle of the nineteenth century their use had practically ceased (Figs. 376 to 381). No domestic implement shows greater variety of design. An early type had the stopper attached to a ring which could be worn on the finger (376). Hogarth shows Father Time wearing one of this kind and smoking a 'Churchwarden' pipe. Another unusual form is shown in Fig. 381. The stem or handle is a small box, the lid being a cribbage board. Inside the box are two compartments, one holding a complete set of dominoes and the other some dice. The press is cross-hatched, which was often the case in later stoppers as they were also used as wafer seals. The press of the early tobacco stoppers is quite small, and gradually increased in diameter as the pipe bowls became larger. They were made of cast brass, bronze, pewter, lead, silver and in many non-metallic substances.

The use of metal tobacco pipes was never very general, as they were hot smoking and expensive. They were made in sheet iron, cast iron, brass, steel and silver. Some early examples are in Belfast Museum (Figs. 382 to 384). The 'Churchwarden' type were made in both steel and silver, with an eighteen-inch stem in three or four sections, which fitted in a case of convenient size to be carried in the pocket (387). In an account of goods belonging to the Company of Coopers, of Kingston-upon-Hull, under the date of 1686, there occurs the following entry:

'Itm Silver tobacco pipe, the gift of Mathew Craven.'

In the early part of the nineteenth century, metal tobacco pipes were used in the hunting field, but owing to accidents occurring by men having falls while smoking, they were abandoned for pipes of clay.

Among articles of tin ware of the early nineteenth century is the pipe case (385). This accommodates a short clay pipe of the cutty variety, and in form takes the lines of a pipe and is similar to the earlier Dutch cases of wood. Another kind is oblong, and with this a place is provided for both tobacco and phosphorous matches, which dates it as not earlier than the middle of the nineteenth century (386).

Smoking mixtures and cut tobaccos are a comparative recent luxury, the old form of retail tobacco being the whole dried leaf, and, later, cake or twist; all of which had to be cut up in fine slices and rubbed between the hands before it was fit for use. An implement for cutting tobacco has the blade attached to a wooden slab, usually maple, about six inches square, the end of the blade being hinged to an upright pin which swivels and allows it to be moved up and down, and also to travel in a quarter circle over the cutting surface (Fig. 389). A rather more elaborate example has a mahogany base standing on four small brass feet (388).

Spills, owing to the introduction of the cheap safety match, have now almost disappeared; they were at one time the most usual form of pipe lighter. A spill-making machine was brought out by the Preston Juniors, probably early in the nineteenth century, and may still be seen, or could until recently, on the counter of some old village inn (Fig. 391). It is formed of a heavy piece of iron, with a channel in the top; at one end is a steel blade, fixed and adjusted as the blade of a moulding plane. To make a spill a piece of wood, preferably soft pine, about half an inch wide, is driven by the hand along the channel towards the blade, which cuts off a shaving in the form of a spiral. These spills were often placed in stands made of sheet iron tube, about nine inches long with a circular base (Fig. 390).

Pipe kilns are wrought-iron racks used in the process of cleaning clay pipes. They are usually made with three rings connected by a flat bar top and bottom, with a ring at top to form a handle; the frame standing upon four squat legs. They were blacksmith made and it is very seldom one finds two of quite the same pattern. These racks of varying design are shown in Figs. 392 to 395. Those in Figs. 392 and 393 follow the usual form but have two, and two and a half rings respectively. Fig. 394 is very exceptional being made of light sectioned iron which forms a square cage for the pipes. This example is in the Sussex Archaeological Society's collection at the Anne of Cleeves House Museum, Lewes, where there are many examples of domestic ironwork. When the pipes became foul with tobacco juice they were not thrown away, but were laid, as many as two or three dozen at a time, in a rack and then placed in a very hot oven until thoroughly baked, when they would be taken out quite clean and more agreeable to smoke than a new pipe. The baking did not always take place at home, but sometimes at the bakers, who made it a business to collect the pipes. This was still being done about the middle of the nineteenth century at the little village of Holmwood, near Dorking in Surrey.

These kilns also served to hold pipes which were in no need of baking. Another type of pipe rack consists of three rings of thin sheet iron with a candle nozzle attached to the centre ring; this rack is supported by six legs with a tray at the base; the two middle legs have conical sockets attached to hold spills (Fig. 396). This was quite a standard type of Smoker's Companion during the eighteenth and nineteenth centuries.

Snuff taking has been practised in this country from the beginning of the seventeenth century, at which time (and for many years afterwards) individuals made their own snuff, either by toasting the tobacco leaf and then grinding it down in a kind of small mortar called a snuff-mill, or rubbing the tobacco plug upon a metal grater similar to, though smaller than, a nutmeg grater (page 61), which is called a snuff-rasp or tobacco rape. It is impossible to determine the date these instruments were first used in this country, but there are existing examples dating from the latter half of the seventeenth century. A treatise, written in 1682 under the title of *The Natural History of Coffee, Thee, Chocolate, and Tobacco*, states that 'The Irishmen do most commonly powder their tobacco and snuff it up their nostrils, which some of our Englishmen do, and often chew and swollow it.' The common type of rasp consists of a long shallow trough covered by a perforated grater. At the small end of the trough is a shallow cup. The tobacco is grated on the rasp, the dust falling into the trough which is then shaken through a small hole into the cup from whence it is carried to the nose by finger and thumb.

70

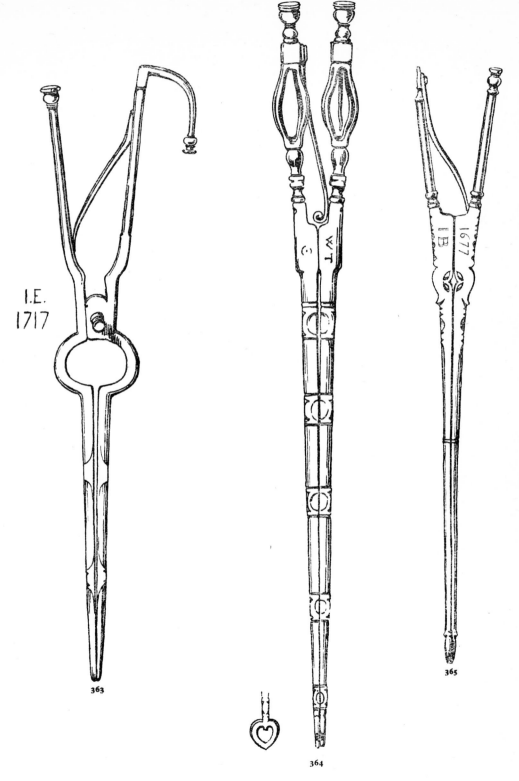

I.E.
1717

363

364

365

## WROUGHT-STEEL PIPE TONGS

363. DATED 1717. *Brighton Museum*      364. 18TH CENTURY. *Guildhall Museum*
365. DATED 1677. *The late L. G. Russell-Davies bequest*

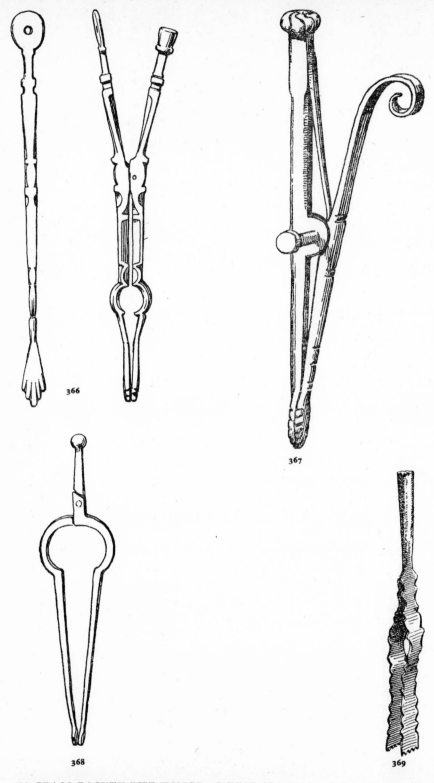

366. BRASS POCKET PIPE TONGS. *Guildhall Museum*
367. WROUGHT-STEEL POCKET PIPE TONGS. *Victoria & Albert Museum*
368. BRASS POCKET PIPE TONGS. *London Museum*
369. WROUGHT-STEEL POCKET PIPE TONGS. *Author's collection*

370. CAST-IRON CASKET TYPE TOBACCO BOX, 18TH CENTURY. Width 5½ ins. overall
371. CIRCULAR LEAD TOBACCO BOX, 18TH CENTURY. Width 4¾ ins. overall

372, 373. CAST-LEAD TOBACCO
BOXES, LATE 18TH CENTURY.
*Mr. C. M. Escaré's collection*

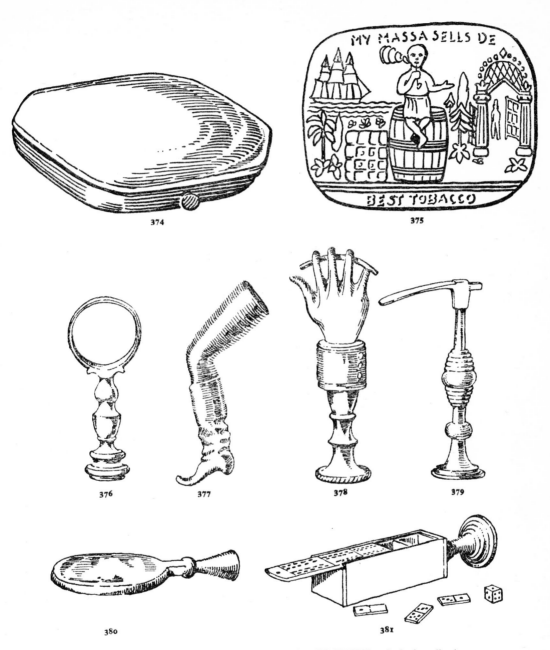

374. STEEL POCKET TOBACCO BOX, LATE 18TH CENTURY. *Author's collection*
375. STEEL POCKET TOBACCO BOX, EARLY 19TH CENTURY. *Mr. C. M. Escaré*
376. BRASS FINGER-RING TOBACCO STOPPER, EARLY 18TH CENTURY. *Author's collection*
377. LEAD TOBACCO STOPPER, 18TH CENTURY. *Author's collection*
378. BRASS TOBACCO STOPPER, 18TH CENTURY. *Author's collection*
379. BRASS TOBACCO STOPPER, 18TH CENTURY. *Mr. C. M. Escaré*
380. BRASS COIN TOBACCO STOPPER, EARLY 18TH CENTURY. *Guildhall Museum*
381. BRASS DOMINO BOX TOBACCO STOPPER, EARLY 19TH CENTURY. *Author's collection*

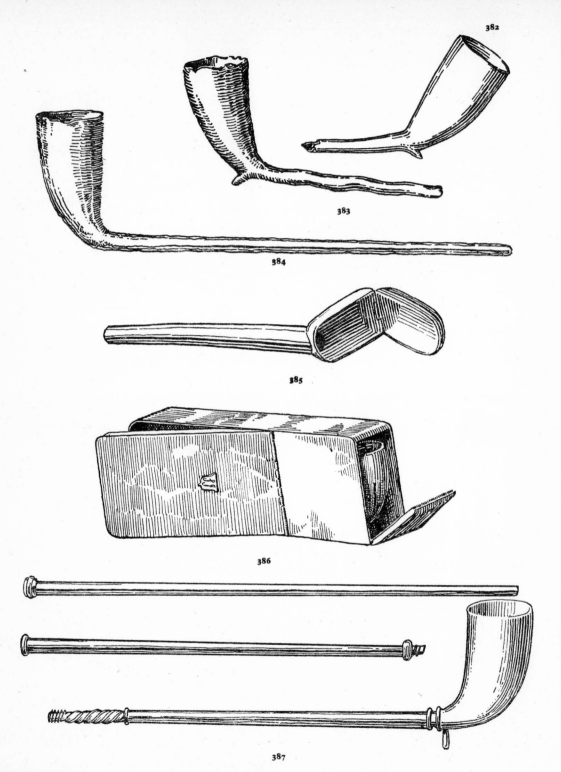

382. CAST-BRASS TOBACCO PIPE, 18TH CENTURY
383. CAST-IRON TOBACCO PIPE, 18TH CENTURY
384. WROUGHT-IRON TOBACCO PIPE, 18TH CENTURY
    382–384. *From Public Art Gallery and Museums, Belfast*
385. TIN PIPE CASE, 19TH CENTURY. *Author's collection*
386. TIN PIPE AND TOBACCO BOX, 19TH CENTURY. *Author's collection*
387. STEEL 'CHURCHWARDEN' TOBACCO PIPE IN THREE SECTIONS. *From an illustration in an 18th century Trade Catalogue in the Victoria & Albert Museum*

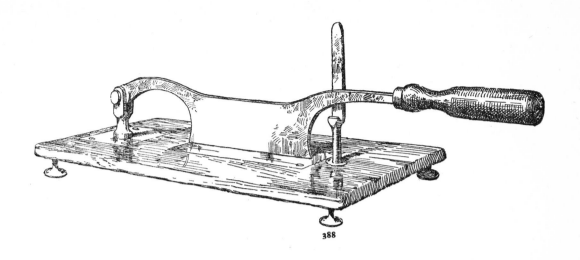

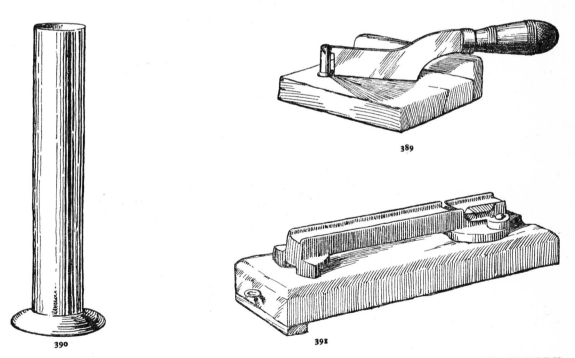

388. TOBACCO CUTTER WITH STEEL BLADE ON MAHOGANY STAND, LATE 18TH CENTURY.
 *Author's collection*
389. TOBACCO CUTTER, STEEL BLADE ON MAPLE STAND. *The late L. G. Russell-Davies bequest*
390. SPILL STAND IN SHEET IRON, EARLY 19TH CENTURY. *The late L. G. Russell-Davies bequest*
391. SPILL CUTTING MACHINE, EARLY 19TH CENTURY. *Author's collection*

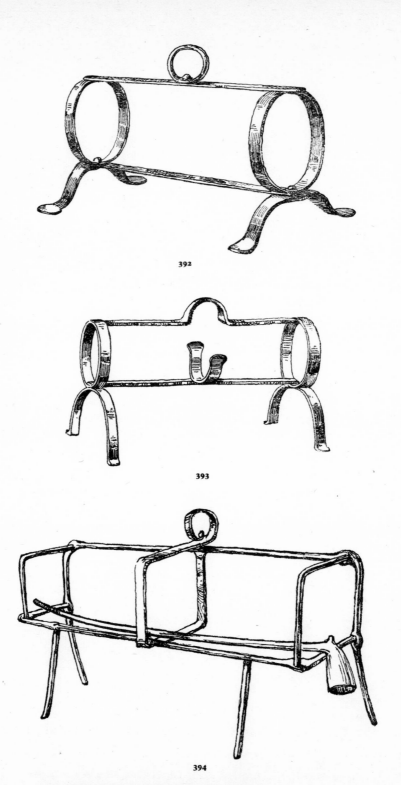

392. TWO-RING PIPE KILN. *From Sussex*
393. TWO-AND-A-HALF RING PIPE KILN. *From Sussex*
394. PIPE KILN. *From Sussex*

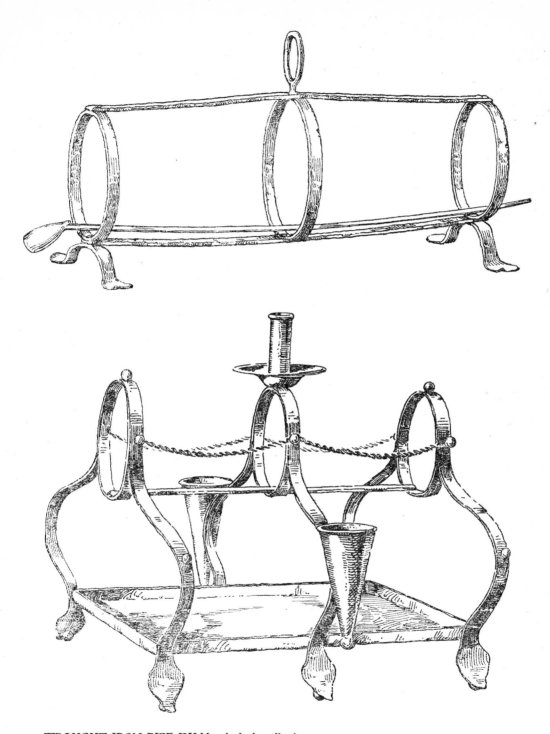

395. WROUGHT-IRON PIPE KILN. *Author's collection*
396. PIPE STAND AND SMOKER'S COMPANION, 18TH CENTURY. *Victoria & Albert Museum*

# PART FIVE
# MISCELLANEOUS

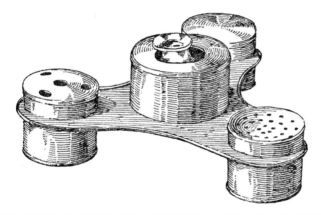

INK STAND IN SHEET IRON, JAPANNED, EARLY 19TH CENTURY
*Victoria & Albert Museum*

# PART FIVE

# MISCELLANEOUS

A DOOR STOP OF unusual and striking design is shown in Fig. 397. A highly stylised lion clasping a circular object between its front paws forms the stop. The handle is of flat wrought iron with zig-zag incised ornament which is cast into the back of the lion much as the billet bars of the late eighteenth century fire-dogs shown in Figs. 14 and 16.

Among the various other articles which cannot be included in any of the foregoing parts are corkscrews. An example of the late seventeenth century, now in the Victoria and Albert Museum, is of pierced steel, the handle being a quatrefoil, a form of decoration common to this class of metalwork which obtained well into the next century. The screw is protected by an openwork cylindrical shield (Fig. 401). The majority of eighteenth-century corkscrews were for pocket use, and they were made in large quantities, an article of this kind being an essential part of a gentleman's equipment. The screw was protected by a sheath case, some of the brass examples having the handle in the shape of a signet ring (399). Towards the end of the eighteenth century they were being turned out in polished steel, the sheath slipping through a top ring in the stem to form the handle (398, 400, and 402).

These articles, together with several other types here illustrated, were known as 'steel toys,' and were produced by manufacturers who advertised their goods as such. The term seems to have included any small steel article that was used as an assistant. The manufacturers of these articles issued catalogues illustrated by engravings, which were used by their bagmen or agents in obtaining orders from the retailers. A collection of these trade catalogues, or pattern books, are to be seen in the Department of Engravings, Illustration, and Design in the Victoria and Albert Museum, catalogued under 'Old English Pattern Books of the Metal Trades.'

Nut crackers were made on two distinct principles, the most primitive being a thumbscrew, made either in some hard close-grained wood or steel. Two of the latter are shown in Figs. 403 and 404, dating from the seventeenth century. This kind was abandoned for the lever design, the earlier form cracking the nut on the far side of the hinge after the manner of pinchers. They are made of delicately wrought steel, the handle finishing in a knob in the form of acorns or, less frequently, tobacco stoppers (407 and 408). The modern design has as its prototype the small brass examples shown in 405 and 406. These form a distinct variety of the mid-eighteenth century: the decoration shows great similarity, consisting of bowed and balustered handles and incised punchmarks (405 and 406).

Other articles which come under the heading of 'steel toys' are key rings (Fig. 410), nail cutters (409), and the small table vices called in the eighteenth-century catalogues 'Ladies' Netting Vices.' These instruments clamped upon a work table. In the earlier vices the work or netting was held by a small hook (Figs. 413 and 414), and those of more recent date by spring jaws, sometimes provided with pincushion and bobbin spindle (Fig. 415). Another favourite pattern was in the form of a dolphin, in cast brass (416), and a cheaper variety in cast iron of similar design.

Some of the earlier designs were very delicate examples of the steel-cutters' art, ornamented by facets and pierced work, with small diamond-cut studs attached to give added richness, similar in treatment to the shoe buckles and brooches of the period.

Although the demand of the eighteenth century caused these household implements to become stereotyped, they still continued to be the work of the artist-craftsman, as is shown by the pair of embroidery scissors shown in Fig. 411, these being descendants of the mediæval weavers shears (412).

In the middle of the nineteenth century, when embroidery and needlework was still a common occupation, table screens were in common use, their purpose being to shade the eyes from the direct glare of the lamp. When out of use, the pleated screen was closed and fitted within the centre stem (Fig. 417).

Spinning wheels have been used from the earliest historical times, and were usually of wood, or wood and iron, the large flywheel some-times being made in that metal. That they were occasionally made entirely of iron is shown by an example in the National Museum of

Antiquities, Edinburgh, which dates from the eighteenth century (Fig. 418).

An ingenious device which proves that port was still being taken seriously as late as the middle of the nineteenth century is the bottle tilter (Fig. 419). The bottle is laid in the cradle, which is slowly tilted by turning the end handle. A half-bottle was accommodated by putting in a false end which is shown in the illustration. The frame was fitted upon a wooden base, the metal work being either of brass or cast iron.

Shoehorns were originally sections of natural horn dressed into convenient shape; during the eighteenth century many patterns were made in brass and in lesser numbers in iron. Three examples are shown in Figs. 420 to 422. Figs. 420 and 421 are of brass, the former being fashioned on traditional lines. Fig. 422 is of wrought iron, and, as the handle suggests, comes from Scotland.

Pattens were a form of clog with the wooden sole raised an inch or an inch and a half from the ground upon an oval iron ring. They were used in this form from the seventeenth century, and served to keep the user's feet free from mud and slush. The illustration (Fig. 423) shows the complete patten with wooden sole and leathern straps and (Fig. 424) the metal work upon which the sole is mounted. The Guildhall Museum exhibits several that were made by William Gardner (1825–1905), last of the London patten-makers.

From the Middle Ages, receptacles for holding ink have been made in various materials such as horn, pewter, glass, etc., and as Society became more cultured and the practice of letter writing extended, inkstands were made to contain, in addition to the ink, sand and wafers, these being necessary before the introduction of blotting-paper and gummed envelopes.

An early nineteenth-century stand of Japanned iron has receptacles for ink, sand, wafers, and a pen stand, the latter holding sand for cleaning corroded quills (see page 71).

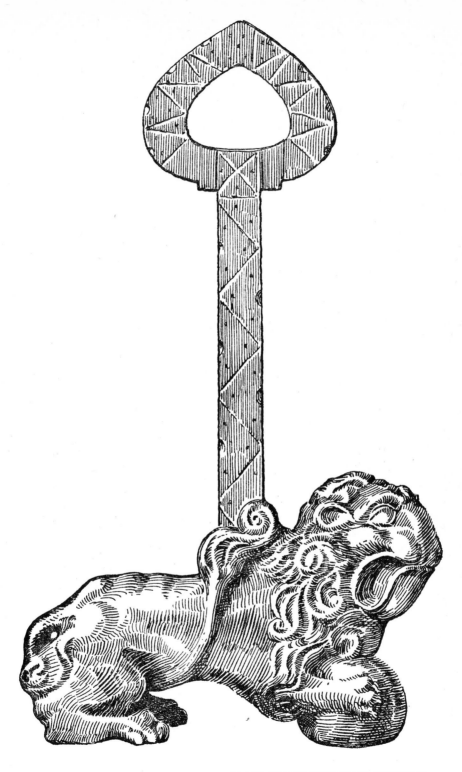

**397.** CAST-IRON DOOR STOP WITH WROUGHT-IRON HANDLE
Height 10 ins. *John Lane collection*

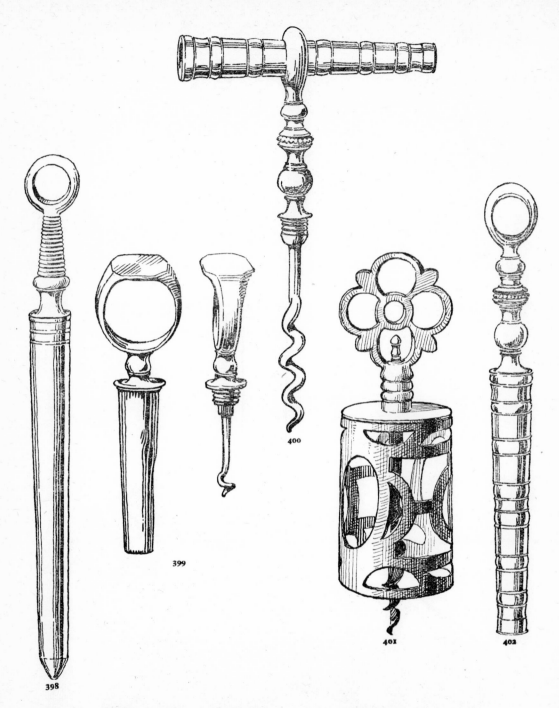

398, 400, 402. CORKSCREWS, STEEL, LATE 18TH CENTURY. *Mr. C. M. Escaré's collection*
399. CORKSCREW, BRASS, LATE 18TH CENTURY. *Mr. C. M. Escaré's collection*
401. CORKSCREW, STEEL, 17TH CENTURY. *Victoria & Albert Museum*

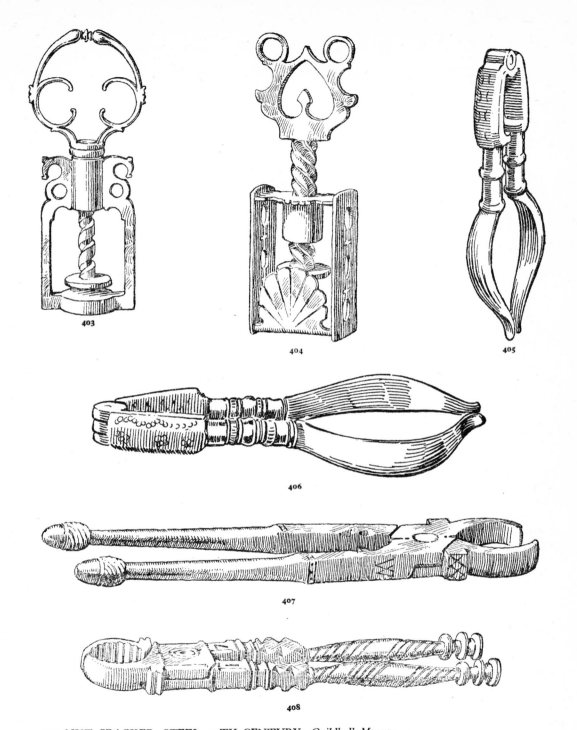

403. NUT CRACKER, STEEL, 17TH CENTURY. *Guildhall Museum*
404. NUT CRACKER, STEEL, 17TH CENTURY. *Victoria & Albert Museum*
405, 406. NUT CRACKERS, BRASS, LATE 18TH CENTURY. *Author's collection*
407. NUT CRACKERS, STEEL, EARLY 18TH CENTURY. *Author's collection*
408. NUT CRACKERS, STEEL, WITH TOBACCO STOPPERS, DATED 1757. *Author's collection*

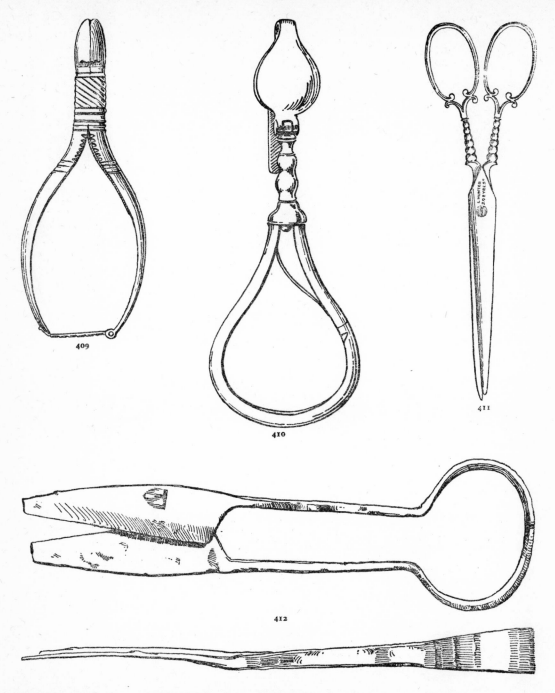

409. NAIL CLIPPERS, STEEL, LATE 18TH CENTURY. *The late L. G. Russell-Davies bequest*
410. KEY RING OR KEEPER, STEEL, LATE 18TH CENTURY. *The late L. G. Russell-Davies bequest*
411. EMBROIDERY SCISSORS, STEEL, LATE 18TH CENTURY. *Author's collection*
412. STEEL SHEARS, 16TH CENTURY. *Author's collection*

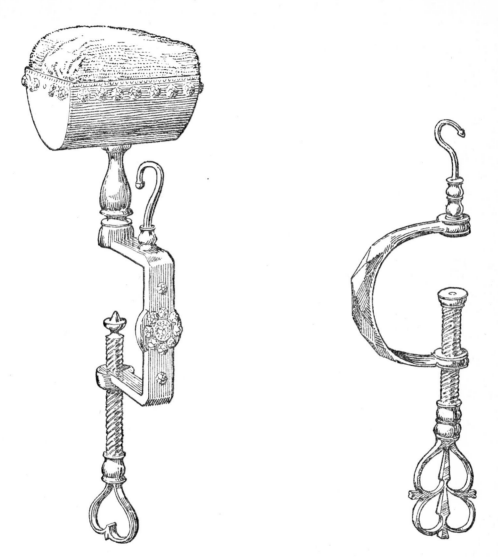

413, 414. NETTING TABLE VICES CUT STEEL, 18TH CENTURY
*Author's collection*

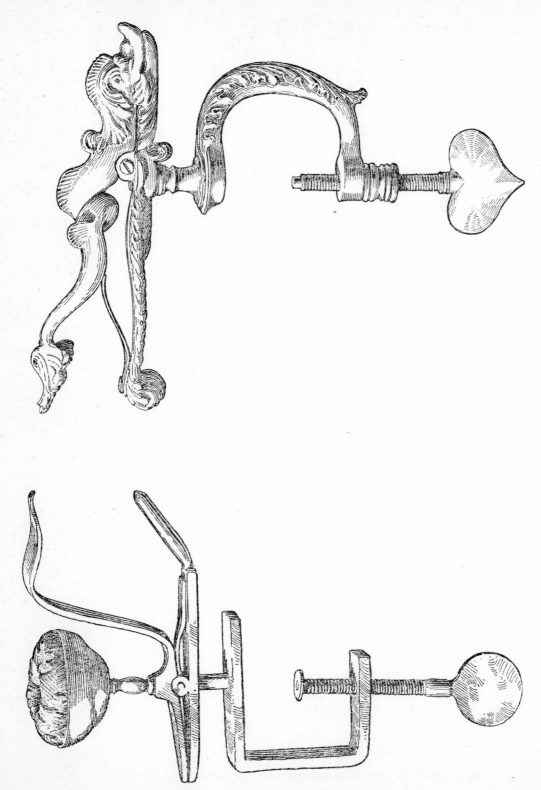

EMBROIDERY TABLE VICES, EARLY 19TH CENTURY

415. Steel          416. Brass. *Author's collection*

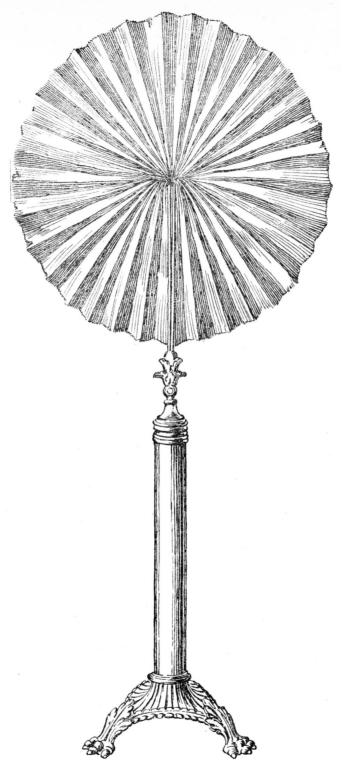

417. TABLE SCREEN, BRASS AND GREEN SILK, MID 19TH CENTURY
Height 18½ ins. *Author's collection*

418. WROUGHT-IRON SPINNING WHEEL: 18TH CENTURY
*National Museum of Antiquities, Edinburgh*

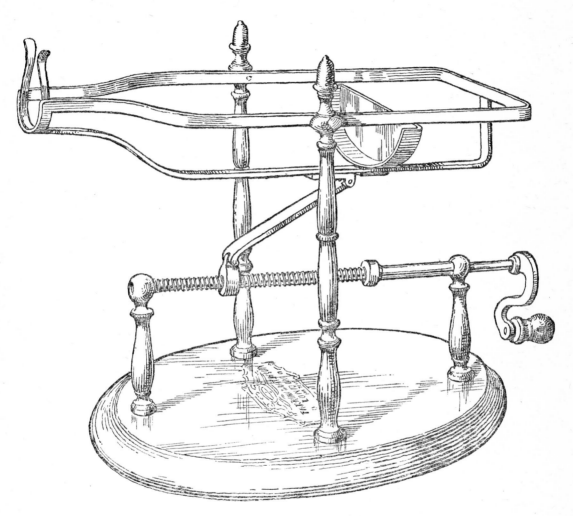

419. PORT TILTER, BRASS, MID 19TH CENTURY
*Author's collection*

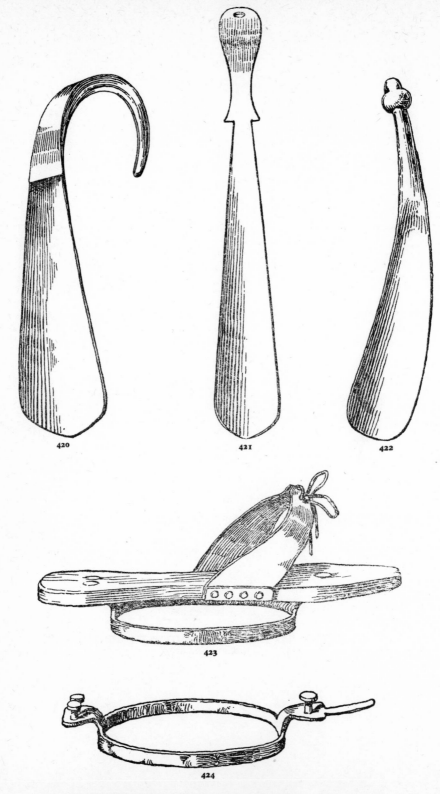

420, 421. SHOEHORNS, BRASS, 18TH CENTURY. *Author's collection*
422. SHOEHORN, WROUGHT IRON, 18TH CENTURY. *Mr. J. A. Butti*
423. PATTEN WITH RECONSTRUCTED SOLE. *Author's collection*
424. PATTEN, WROUGHT-IRON FRAME. *Author's collection*

# SOME EXAMPLES OF AMERICAN COLONIAL IMPLEMENTS

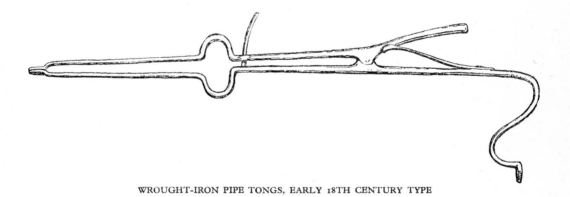

WROUGHT-IRON PIPE TONGS, EARLY 18TH CENTURY TYPE

# SOME EXAMPLES OF
# AMERICAN COLONIAL IMPLEMENTS

THE EARLIEST METAL DOMESTIC IMPLEMENTS used in the Colonies were taken out by the original settlers and it is unlikely to have included anything that was not a strict necessity. As others followed these early adventurers, and as conditions improved, more of these implements found their way to the new country and came to be reproduced by the ever-expanding communities. New conditions of life and mixed nationalities brought about fresh types peculiar to America.

Small change was made in fire implements, and in many of the early houses fireplaces identical in every respect with those in contemporary English kitchens were built, furnished with fire-dogs, spit dogs, chimney cranes, and fire-backs, etc.

The earliest foundry which cast fire-backs was the Saugus Ironworks which must be considered the first important ironworks to remain a long-established concern. Raw material was obtained from a deposit of bog iron, which the settlers discovered near Boston.

A fine example from this foundry is shown in Fig. 426. It is ornamented with the initials of the Pickering family, the date 1660, and movable stamps on the remaining plain surface: an early method used prior to the one-piece carved pattern. The latter are represented in Figs. 427 and 428.

There are many old colonial fireplaces still in existence, carefully preserved. Among the best known is the down-hearth shown in Fig. 425. This is at Mount Vernon, the home of George Washington, which dates from the middle of the eighteenth century. In addition to it being a fireplace well stocked with implements, there is a fine wood spit rack similar in design to those found in many parts of Britain.

The spit dogs at Mount Vernon are of a massive angular design with four hooks on the face of the upright stems in which the spit could revolve at varying heights.

A common feature of American dogs is the flattening out of the stem at the base of the goose neck (Figs. 429 and 430). The small dog in Fig. 431 is one of a pair of creepers, used between the large dogs to give extra ventilation.

Kitchen paraphernalia was mainly on English lines although some later examples show the influence of other European countries.

Meat was roasted upon spits, bottle jacks, and trammels—an adjustable pendant terminating in three hooks (Fig. 435). Dutch ovens also figured in the smaller houses. Meat spits terminating in a crank handle, as those in Mount Vernon kitchen, were turned by hand. Those with a wheel, by weight-driven jacks or smoke jacks. There are authentic records showing that the dog-and-drum principle was not unknown (see Fig. 93).

Among articles of the kitchen which survived until the middle of the nineteenth century, illustrated here are the skewer holders in Figs. 436, 440 to 442, goffering iron in Fig. 437, girdle plate Fig. 439, pastry jigger Fig. 438, all emphasising that in these humble household assistants decoration in some form was ever present but never at the expense of the article's usefulness.

Implements used in front of the open fire are shown in the next plate. Wrought-iron flippers (Figs. 443 and 444) are similar to the English oven slice. Toddy irons or mullers (Figs. 445 and 446) would appear to be peculiar to the homes of the early settlers and to have enjoyed a long term of usefulness.

Down-hearth toasters for both bread (Figs. 447 and 449) and meat (Fig. 448) are American types and, although similar implements were in use in Britain, these all show a distinct colonial feeling. One feature that is very obvious is the use of the twist, which stiffened the light section iron and also had a decorative value.

Fireside implements were made in considerable variety. Pot hooks with adjustable caliper-like hooks to suspend the cauldrons, and the lighter double hook for kettle or bow-handled skillet are shown in Figs. 450 and 451. A small article which seems peculiar to this epoch is the cauldron or pot lifting hook (Fig. 453). The long, shallow trough with shaped handle, shown in Fig. 452, was used to catch dripping fat ; a rare type of implement.

Pewter plates were carried to be warmed in front of the fire in an open-sided, circular container which stood on three forged legs and was lifted by a half-hoop handle (Fig. 454).

As the early settlers were for the most part refined and educated people, it is only reasonable to suppose that they endeavoured to make domestic life correspond to the conditions to which they were accustomed. Artificial lighting would be amongst the first problems. They found the native Indians using strips of resinous pine, similar to the Scottish candle-fir. This was used and continued to be used in the humbler dwellings, but was not favoured, as it was necessary to burn it within the hearth opening owing to the great volume of smoke.

Lamps on the crusie principle, burning fish oil (Fig. 466), were identical in every way with the Scottish prototype, having two valves or cups, the inner movable valve containing the oil and the lower or fixed valve supported the container and caught the oil as it syphoned over from the semi-recumbent wick. They date from the seventeenth and eighteenth centuries.

The French type of single valve lamp was also used in the lesser houses (Fig. 467). The cup or valve contained a thin oil, probably vegetable, in which floated a wick supported by a cork float protected on the top face by an exceedingly thin metal disc (Fig. 468).

From the open valve lamp evolved the closed Betty container shown in Fig. 458. And later, when camphene oil was introduced about the middle of the nineteenth century, lamps with one or more long, verticle burners were made. Camphene was a form of refined turpentine and was highly explosive, and to keep the container cool so as to minimise the risk of accident, the spouts were made longer (Fig. 457). Lamps for burning lard oil were made on similar lines, but with short spouts (Figs. 455 and 456).

A lamp in common use from the end of the eighteenth century, constructed to burn whale oil, was the bull's-eye reading lamp (Fig. 459). They were usually made of pewter with a shade of this metal over the lens.

In the eighteenth century the colonists were producing their own ingredients for making candles. Not only were sufficient cattle raised to enable the making of tallow candles and rushlights, but a vegetable wax was obtained from the fruit of a small bush called the bayberry or candle-berry, which grew in profusion in coastal districts. The fruit ripening in the fall was gathered and boiled in large cauldrons, the fat or wax being skimmed off and clarified, forming a green substance that burnt with a good light and gave a faint but pleasant odour.

Rushlights were made from fat melted in a grisset similar in form to those used in England (Fig. 471).

Candles were dipped or made in tin moulds of the same pattern as those in Figs. 217 and 218. In producing fittings for holding candles the American tinsmith developed his ingenuity and sense of design. Iron being difficult to come by for many years, the tinsmith was obliged to improvise. This was accomplished in the making of pendant candelabra by the use of tin plate together with wood bodies, as shown in Fig. 461, or wholly in metal with double cone body (Fig. 462).

Other appliances were standards with tin bases (Fig. 463), wall sconces in a great number of very attractive designs (Fig. 470), and a great assortment of hand and hanging lanterns (Figs. 472 and 473). With the exception of some of the lanterns, these designs are wholly of American conception.

A type of floor standard that can be traced back to early seventeenth century examples had in their time evolved from the mediaeval iron candle standard shown in Fig. 224. The colonial example in Fig. 465 has the decorative motifs in polished brass, including candle sockets and pans. An adjustable spring controlled candle pendant is shown in Fig. 469.

Fire-making implements are similar to English examples shown in Part Three. The tinder boxes were for the most part plain tinsmithing. The very rare friction wheel tinder box which is illustrated in Fig. 332 is also to be found in American collections.

When comparing colonial with English examples there is in many some slight difference which proclaims their American origin. This can be noticed in tobacco tongs (see page 77), as the design has more movement; the jaws are guided by a quadrant pin similar to the wood tongs shown in Fig. 78.

425. FIREPLACE IN THE KITCHEN AT MOUNT VERNON, THE HOME OF
GEORGE WASHINGTON

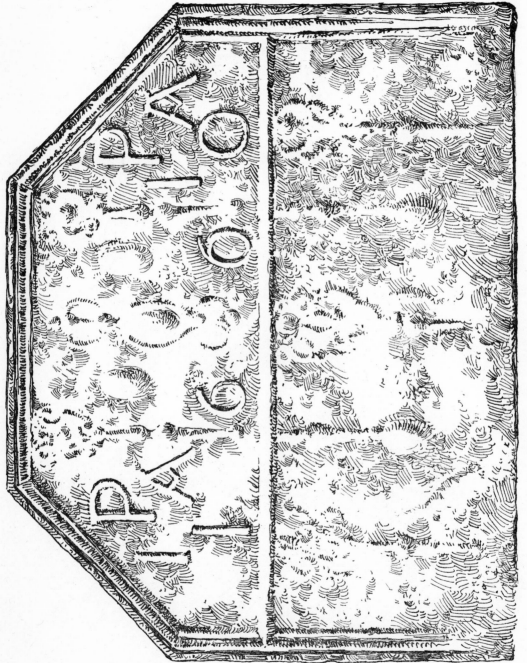

426. CAST-IRON FIRE-BACK OF JOHN AND ALICE PICKERING, DATED 1660
Width 28 ins. *From the Essex Institute collection, Salem*

427. CAST-IRON FIRE-BACK, WITH PORTRAIT OF WASHINGTON, DATED 1788
Width 28 ins. *From the Henry Francis du Pont Museum, Winterthur*
428. CAST-IRON FIRE-BACK, DATED 1781
Width 27 ins. *From the Henry Francis du Pont Museum, Winterthur*

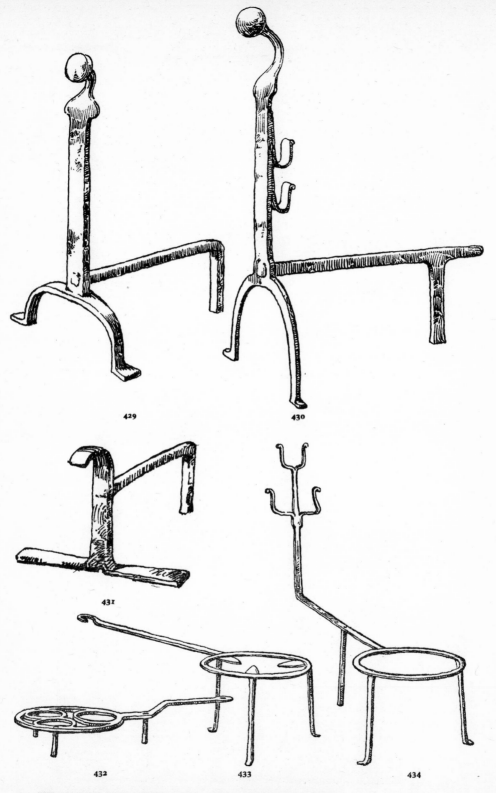

429. WROUGHT-IRON FIRE-DOG, 18TH CENTURY TYPE
430. WROUGHT-IRON SPIT DOG, 18TH CENTURY TYPE
431. CREEPER FIRE-DOG FROM NEW ENGLAND
Height 6 ins. *Charles F. Montgomery collection*
432. WROUGHT-IRON DOWN-HEARTH BAKERY IRON, 18TH CENTURY TYPE
433, 434. WROUGHT-IRON DOWN-HEARTH TRIVETS, 18TH CENTURY TYPES

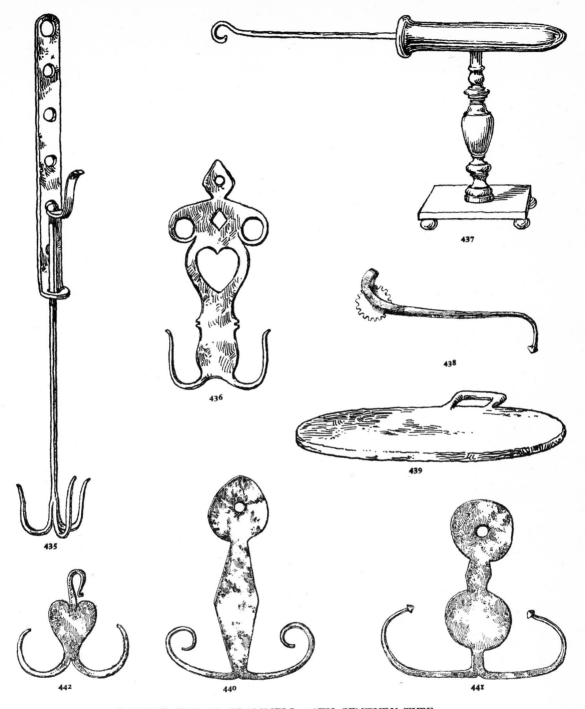

435. DANGLE SPIT OR TRAMMELL, 18TH CENTURY TYPE
436. WROUGHT-IRON SKEWER HOLDER, 17TH–18TH CENTURY TYPE
437. GOFFERING IRON AND HEATER, EARLY 19TH CENTURY TYPE
438. PASTRY JIGGER, 17TH CENTURY. *Charles F. Montgomery collection*
439. GIRDLE PLATE, 18TH CENTURY TYPE
440, 441. SKEWER HOLDERS, 17TH–18TH CENTURY TYPES
*From the Essex Institute collection, Salem*
442. SKEWER HOLDER, 18TH CENTURY
*From the Henry Francis du Pont Museum, Winterthur*

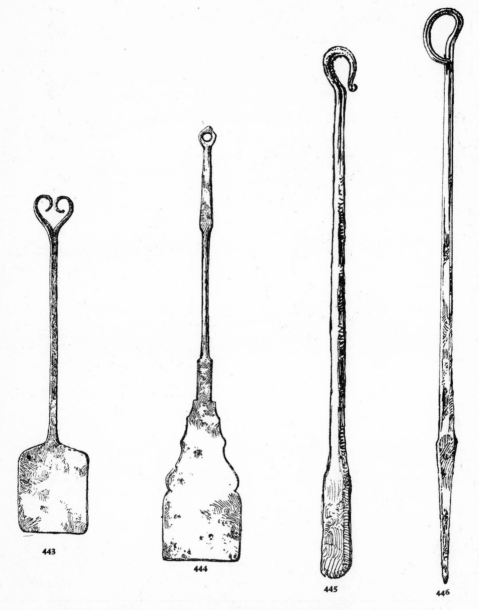

443, 444. WROUGHT-IRON FLIPPERS FROM PENNSYLVANIA
*Charles F. Montgomery collection*
445. TODDY IRON OR MULLER. *Charles F. Montgomery collection*
446. TODDY IRON OR MULLER. *Mr. & Mrs. Roger Bacon collection*

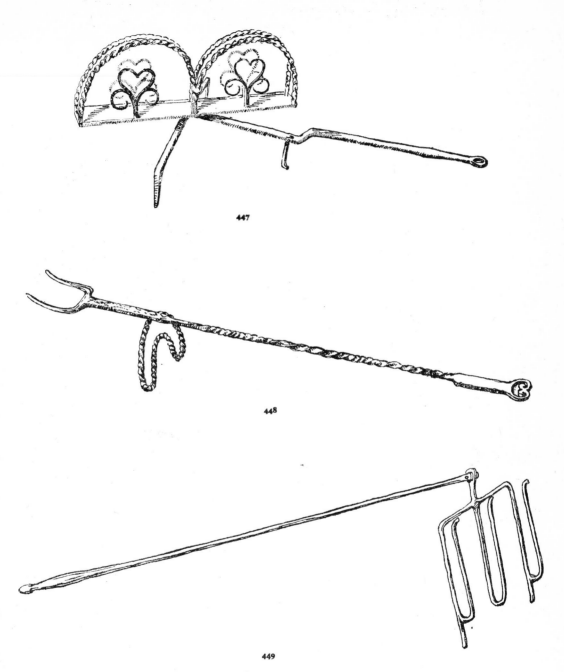

447. DOWN-HEARTH TOASTER WITH REVOLVING RACK FROM NEW ENGLAND,
18TH CENTURY. Handle 14 ins long. *Charles F. Montgomery collection*
448. DOWN-HEARTH TOASTING FORK FROM PENNSYLVANIA. Length 22 ins.
*Charles F. Montgomery collection*
449. DOWN-HEARTH TOASTER, 18TH CENTURY TYPE

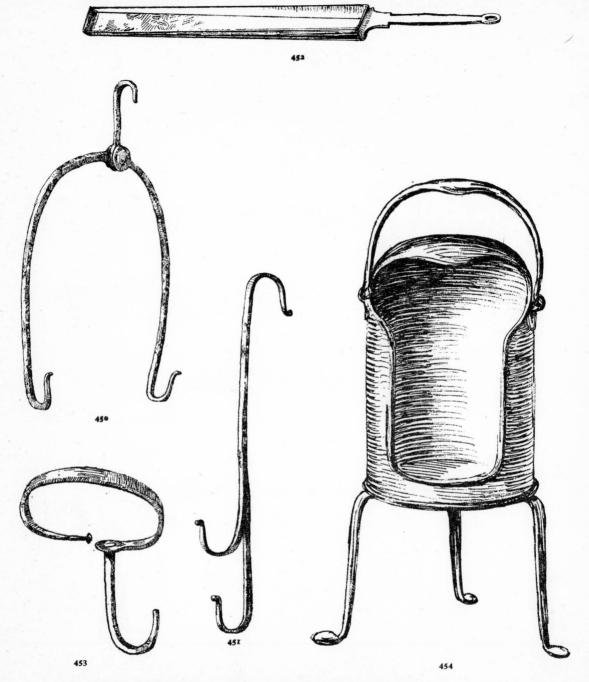

450. HINGE TYPE KETTLE OR POT HOLDER FROM NEW ENGLAND, 17TH–18TH
CENTURY TYPE. *Charles F. Montgomery collection*
451. WROUGHT-IRON POT HOOK FROM NEW ENGLAND. 17 ins. long
*Charles F. Montgomery collection*
452. WROUGHT-IRON GREASE CATCHER TROUGH. Length 18½ ins.
*Mrs. Lucy B. Mitchell collection*
453. KETTLE OR CAULDRON LIFTING HOOK FROM NEW ENGLAND, 18TH
CENTURY. *Charles F. Montgomery collection*
454. PLATE WARMER AND CARRIER, LATE 18TH CENTURY TYPE

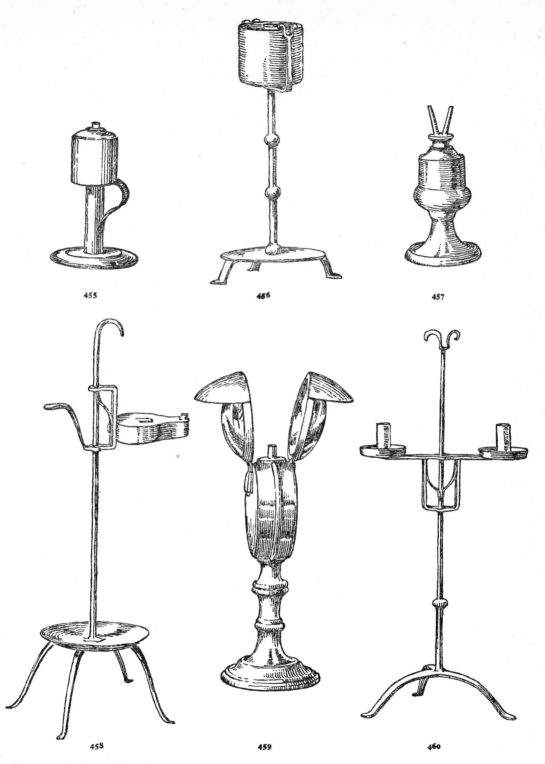

455. TIN WHALE OIL LAMP, EARLY 19TH CENTURY
456. WROUGHT-IRON WHALE OIL LAMP, LATE 18TH CENTURY
457. CAMPHENE LAMP, MID 19TH CENTURY
458. BETTY LAMP ON WROUGHT-IRON STAND, EARLY 19TH CENTURY
459. BULL'S-EYE LAMP IN PEWTER, 19TH CENTURY
460. WROUGHT-IRON TABLE STANDARD WITH SLIDING CARRIER FOR TWO
      CANDLES, 18TH CENTURY TYPE

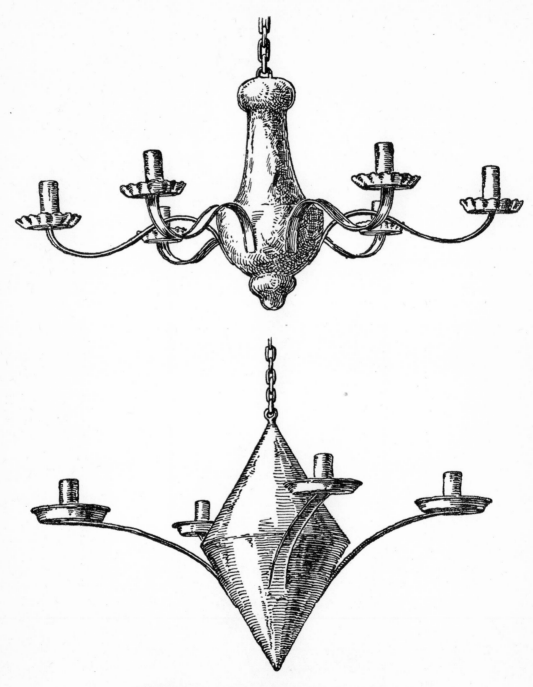

CANDELABRA, LATE 18TH CENTURY TYPES
461. WOOD BODY WITH SIX TIN ARMS AND SOCKETS
462. TIN WITH FOUR BRANCHES

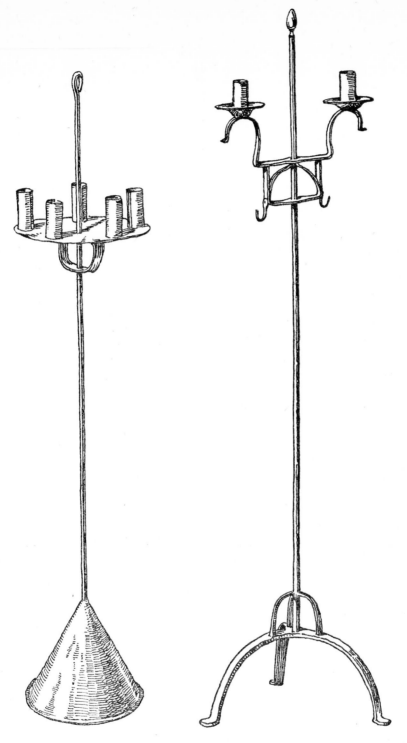

463. FLOOR STANDARD WITH TIN SAND-WEIGHTED BASE AND CARRIER FOR
FIVE CANDLES, EARLY 19TH CENTURY TYPE
464. FLOOR STANDARD OF WROUGHT-IRON WITH TIN CANDLE SOCKETS,
LATE 18TH CENTURY TYPE

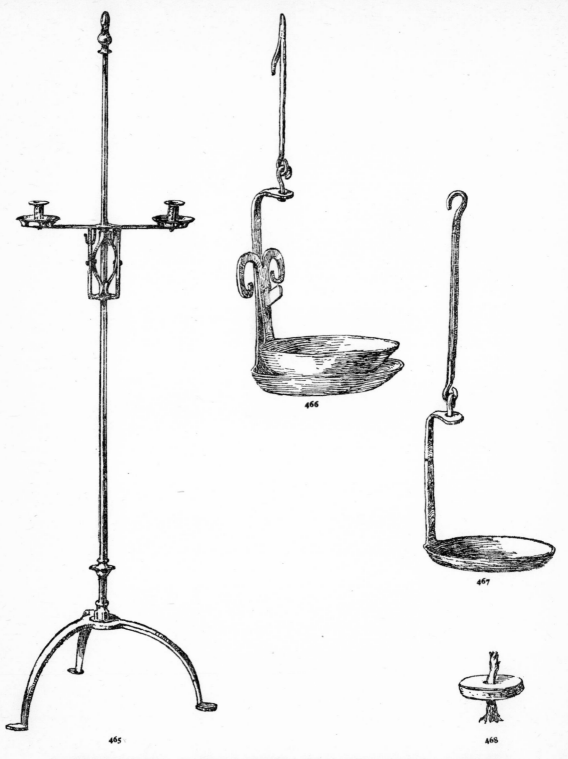

**465.** WROUGHT-IRON FLOOR STANDARD FOR TWO CANDLES FIXED TO
ADJUSTABLE SLIDE. Early 17th century type with brass enrichments. Height 5ft. 5ins.
*Henry Francis du Pont Museum, Winterthur*

**466.** DOUBLE VALVE OIL LAMP, SCOTTISH TYPE FOR FISH OIL, 17TH CENTURY

**467.** SINGLE VALVE OIL LAMP, FRENCH TYPE FOR VEGETABLE OIL, 18TH
CENTURY

**468.** FLOATING WICK, ¾-in. diameter

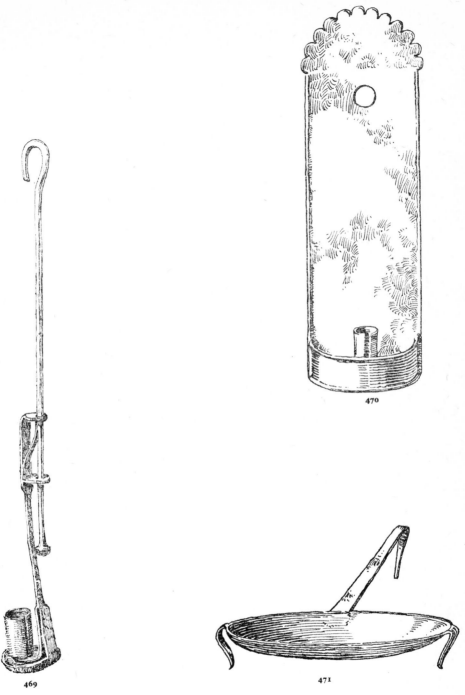

469. IRON ADJUSTABLE CANDLE PENDANT FROM NEW ENGLAND. Length 18 ins.
*Charles F. Montgomery collection*
470. TIN WALL SCONCE, EARLY 19TH CENTURY TYPE
471. WROUGHT-IRON GRISSETT, 17TH CENTURY TYPE

472. FIVE-SIDED HAND CANDLE LANTERN, EARLY 19TH CENTURY TYPE
473. HAND LANTERN WITH TIN CAP AND BASE FOR OIL, EARLY 19TH CENTURY
TYPE

# INDEX

*(bold figures refer to illustrations)*